www.EffortlessMath.com

... So Much More Online!

✓ FREE Math lessons

✓ More Math learning books!

✓ Mathematics Worksheets

✓ Online Math Tutors

Need a PDF version of this book?

Send email to: info@EffortlessMath.com

AFOQT Math Preparation Exercise Book

A Comprehensive Math Workbook and Two Full-Length AFOQT Math Practice Tests

By

Reza Nazari

& Sam Mest

Copyright © 2019

Reza Nazari & Sam Mest

All inquiries should be addressed to:

info@effortlessMath.com

www.EffortlessMath.com

Published by: Effortless Math Education

www.EffortlessMath.com

Description

AFOQT Math Preparation Exercise Book provides test takers with an in-depth focus on the math portion of the exam, helping them master the math skills that students find the most troublesome. It is designed to address the needs of AFOQT test takers who must have a working knowledge of basic Math.

This comprehensive AFOQT Math Workbook contains many exciting and unique features to help you score higher on the AFOQT Math test, including:

- Content 100% aligned with the 2019 AFOQT test

- Prepared by AFOQT Math experts

- Complete coverage of all AFOQT Math topics which you will need to ace the test

- Over 2,500 additional AFOQT math practice questions with answers

- 2 complete AFOQT Math practice tests (featuring new question types) with detailed answers

AFOQT Math Preparation Exercise Book is an incredibly useful tool for those AFOQT test takers who want to review core content areas, brush-up in math, discover their strengths and weaknesses, and achieve their best scores on the AFOQT test.

Contents

Section 1: Arithmetic 8

  Chapter 1: Fractions and Decimals 9

    Simplifying Fractions 10

    Adding and Subtracting Fraction 11

    Multiplying and Dividing Fractions 12

    Adding Mixed Numbers 13

    Subtract Mixed Numbers 14

    Multiplying Mixed Numbers 15

    Dividing Mixed Numbers 16

    Comparing Decimals 17

    Rounding Decimals 18

    Adding and Subtracting Decimals 19

    Multiplying and Dividing Decimals 20

    Converting Between Fractions, Decimals and Mixed Numbers 21

    Factoring Numbers 22

    Greatest Common Factor 23

    Least Common Multiple 24

    Answers of Worksheets 25

  Chapter 2: Real Numbers and Integers 30

    Adding and Subtracting Integers 31

    Multiplying and Dividing Integers 32

    Ordering Integers and Numbers 33

    Arrange, Order, and Comparing Integers 34

    Order of Operations 35

    Mixed Integer Computations 36

    Integers and Absolute Value 37

    Answers of Worksheets 38

  Chapter 3: Proportions and Ratios 41

    Writing Ratios 42

    Simplifying Ratios 43

    Create a Proportion 44

Similar Figures 45

Simple Interest 46

Ratio and Rates Word Problems 47

Answers of Worksheets 48

Chapter 4: Percent 50

Percentage Calculations 51

Converting Between Percent, Fractions, and Decimals 52

Percent Problems 53

Find What Percentage a Number Is of Another 54

Find a Percentage of a Given Number 55

Percent of Increase and Decrease 56

Markup, Discount, and Tax 57

Answers of Worksheets 58

Section 2: Algebra 60

Chapter 5: Algebraic Expressions 61

Expressions and Variables 62

Simplifying Variable Expressions 63

Simplifying Polynomial Expressions 64

The Distributive Property 65

Evaluating One Variable 66

Evaluating Two Variables 67

Combining like Terms 68

Answers of Worksheets 69

Chapter 6: Equations and Inequalities 72

One–Step Equations 73

One–Step Equation Word Problems 74

Two–Step Equations 75

Two–Step Equation Word Problems 76

Multi–Step Equations 77

Graphing Single–Variable Inequalities 78

One–Step Inequalities 79

Multi-Step Inequalities 80

Answers of Worksheets 81

Chapter 7: Systems of Equations 84

    Solving Systems of Equations by Substitution 85

    Solving Systems of Equations by Elimination 86

    Systems of Equations Word Problems 87

    Answers of Worksheets 88

Chapter 8: Linear Functions 89

    Finding Slope 90

    Graphing Lines Using Slope–Intercept Form 91

    Graphing Lines Using Standard Form 92

    Writing Linear Equations 93

    Graphing Linear Inequalities 94

    Finding Midpoint 95

    Finding Distance of Two Points 96

    Slope and Rate of Change 97

    Find the Slope, x–intercept and y–intercept 98

    Write an equation from a graph 99

    Slope–intercept Form 100

    Point–slope Form 101

    Equations of Horizontal and Vertical Lines 102

    Equation of Parallel or Perpendicular Lines 103

    Answers of Worksheets 104

Chapter 9: Monomials and Polynomials 111

    Writing Polynomials in Standard Form 112

    Simplifying Polynomials 113

    Add and Subtract monomials 114

    Multiplying Monomials 115

    Multiplying and Dividing Monomials 116

    GCF of Monomials 117

    Powers of monomials 118

    Multiplying a Polynomial and a Monomial 119

    Multiplying Binomials 120

    Factoring Trinomials 121

    Answers of Worksheets 122

Chapter 10: Exponents and Radicals..128

   Multiplication Property of Exponents..129

   Division Property of Exponents..130

   Powers of Products and Quotients..131

   Zero and Negative Exponents..132

   Writing Scientific Notation..133

   Square Roots...134

   Answers of Worksheets...135

Section 3: Geometry and Statistics...138

Chapter 11: Plane Figures...139

   Transformations: Translations, Rotations, and Reflections...............................140

   The Pythagorean Theorem 141

   Area of Triangles..142

   Perimeter of Polygon...143

   Area and Circumference of Circles...144

   Area of Squares, Rectangles, and Parallelograms...145

   Area of Trapezoids..146

   Answers of Worksheets...147

Chapter 12: Solid Figures..149

   Volume of Cubes and Rectangle Prisms...150

   Surface Area of Cubes..151

   Surface Area of a Prism..152

   Volume of Pyramids and Cones 153

   Answers of Worksheets...154

Chapter 13: Statistics...155

   Mean, Median, Mode, and Range of the Given Data 156

   Box and Whisker Plot...157

   Bar Graph 158

   Stem–And–Leaf Plot...159

   The Pie Graph or Circle Graph..160

   Scatter Plots 161

   Answers of Worksheets...162

Chapter 14: Probability...168

Probability of Simple Events 169

Experimental Probability... 170

Factorials 171

Combinations and Permutations 172

Answers of Worksheets 173

AFOQT Test Review.. 174

AFOQT Math Practice Tests 175

AFOQT Math Test 1 Arithmetic Reasoning 178

AFOQT Math Practice Test 1 Mathematics Knowledge 184

AFOQT Math Test 2 Arithmetic Reasoning 190

AFOQT Math Practice Test 2 Mathematics Knowledge 196

FAOQT Mathematics Practice Tests Answers and Explanations.. 201

Send email to: info@EffortlessMath.com 215

Section 1: Arithmetic

- *Fractions and Decimals*

- *Real Numbers and Integers*

- *Proportions and Ratios*

- *Percent*

Chapter 1:

Fractions and Decimals

Topics that you'll learn in this part:

- ✓ Simplifying Fractions
- ✓ Adding and Subtracting Fractions
- ✓ Multiplying and Dividing Fractions
- ✓ Adding Mixed Numbers
- ✓ Subtract Mixed Numbers
- ✓ Multiplying Mixed Numbers
- ✓ Dividing Mixed Numbers
- ✓ Comparing Decimals
- ✓ Rounding Decimals

- ✓ Adding and Subtracting Decimals
- ✓ Multiplying and Dividing Decimals
- ✓ Converting Between Fractions, Decimals and Mixed Numbers
- ✓ Factoring Numbers
- ✓ Greatest Common Factor
- ✓ Least Common Multiple
- ✓ Divisibility Rules

Simplifying Fractions

✎*Simplify the fractions.*

1) $\dfrac{33}{54} =$

2) $\dfrac{12}{15} =$

3) $\dfrac{18}{27} =$

4) $\dfrac{12}{16} =$

5) $\dfrac{26}{78} =$

6) $\dfrac{10}{40} =$

7) $\dfrac{20}{45} =$

8) $\dfrac{18}{36} =$

9) $\dfrac{40}{100} =$

10) $\dfrac{6}{54} =$

11) $\dfrac{15}{27} =$

12) $\dfrac{15}{20} =$

13) $\dfrac{20}{32} =$

14) $\dfrac{26}{32} =$

15) $\dfrac{15}{75} =$

16) $\dfrac{40}{70} =$

17) $\dfrac{24}{48} =$

18) $\dfrac{35}{84} =$

19) $\dfrac{15}{40} =$

20) $\dfrac{15}{60} =$

21) $\dfrac{30}{54} =$

✎*Solve*

22) Which of the following fractions equal to $\dfrac{4}{5}$? _____

A. $\dfrac{64}{75}$

B. $\dfrac{92}{115}$

C. $\dfrac{60}{85}$

D. $\dfrac{160}{220}$

23) Which of the following fractions equal to $\dfrac{3}{7}$? _____

A. $\dfrac{63}{147}$

B. $\dfrac{75}{182}$

C. $\dfrac{54}{140}$

D. $\dfrac{39}{98}$

24) Which of the following fractions equal to $\dfrac{7}{15}$? _____

A. $\dfrac{33}{56}$

B. $\dfrac{25}{85}$

C. $\dfrac{42}{90}$

D. $\dfrac{23}{72}$

Adding and Subtracting Fraction

✎ Add fractions.

1) $\dfrac{3}{5} + \dfrac{2}{4} =$

4) $\dfrac{7}{8} + \dfrac{5}{3} =$

7) $\dfrac{2}{4} + \dfrac{2}{7} =$

2) $\dfrac{2}{7} + \dfrac{3}{5} =$

5) $\dfrac{3}{5} + \dfrac{1}{10} =$

8) $\dfrac{4}{3} + \dfrac{1}{4} =$

3) $\dfrac{2}{7} + \dfrac{1}{4} =$

6) $\dfrac{2}{9} + \dfrac{2}{3} =$

9) $\dfrac{9}{21} + \dfrac{3}{7} =$

✎ Subtract fractions.

10) $\dfrac{3}{5} - \dfrac{1}{5} =$

13) $\dfrac{5}{8} - \dfrac{1}{5} =$

16) $\dfrac{5}{6} - \dfrac{8}{18} =$

11) $\dfrac{4}{5} - \dfrac{3}{6} =$

14) $\dfrac{4}{5} - \dfrac{6}{10} =$

17) $\dfrac{5}{12} - \dfrac{18}{24} =$

12) $\dfrac{1}{3} - \dfrac{1}{6} =$

15) $\dfrac{12}{20} - \dfrac{3}{10} =$

18) $\dfrac{1}{5} - \dfrac{1}{8} =$

✎ Solve.

19) A city worker is painting a stripe down the center of Main Street. Main Street is $\dfrac{8}{10}$ mile long. The worker painted $\dfrac{3}{10}$ mile of the street. How much of the street painting is left?

20) From a board 8 feet in length, Tim cut to $2\dfrac{1}{3}$ foot book shelves. How much of the board remained?

21) While taking inventory at his pastry shop, Eddie realizes that he had $\dfrac{1}{2}$ of a box of baking powder yesterday, but the supply is now down to $\dfrac{1}{8}$ of a box. How much more baking powder did Eddie have yesterday?

Multiplying and Dividing Fractions

✎ *Multiply fractions. Then simplify.*

1) $\frac{2}{7} \times \frac{5}{9} =$

2) $\frac{2}{4} \times \frac{3}{7} =$

3) $\frac{1}{2} \times \frac{4}{7} =$

4) $\frac{2}{3} \times \frac{1}{5} =$

5) $\frac{9}{10} \times \frac{2}{3} =$

6) $\frac{5}{7} \times \frac{9}{11} =$

7) $\frac{6}{9} \times \frac{2}{6} =$

8) $\frac{3}{4} \times \frac{2}{5} =$

9) $\frac{4}{7} \times \frac{7}{9} =$

✎ *Divide fractions. Simplify if necessary.*

10) $\frac{1}{9} \div \frac{3}{5} =$

11) $\frac{1}{6} \div \frac{2}{7} =$

12) $\frac{6}{9} \div \frac{7}{9} =$

13) $\frac{12}{9} \div \frac{13}{8} =$

14) $\frac{3}{20} \div \frac{5}{10} =$

15) $\frac{1}{5} \div \frac{3}{2} =$

16) $\frac{4}{6} \div \frac{3}{6} =$

17) $\frac{11}{24} \div \frac{1}{12} =$

18) $\frac{7}{14} \div \frac{3}{9} =$

19) $\frac{35}{14} \div \frac{7}{14} =$

20) $\frac{63}{15} \div \frac{14}{20} =$

21) $\frac{110}{50} \div \frac{11}{20} =$

✎ *Solve.*

22) Vera is using her phone. Its battery life is down to $\frac{2}{5}$, and it drains another $\frac{1}{9}$ every hour. How many hours will her battery last?

    A. $\frac{25}{9}$ B. $\frac{18}{5}$ C. $\frac{16}{5}$ D. 5

23) A factory uses $\frac{1}{3}$ of a barrel of raisins in each batch of granola bars. Yesterday, the factory used $\frac{2}{3}$ of a barrel of raisins. How many batches of granola bars did the factory make yesterday?

    A. $\frac{1}{3}$ B. $\frac{2}{3}$ C. $\frac{3}{2}$ D. 2

Adding Mixed Numbers

✎ *Add.*

1) $2\frac{1}{4} + 1\frac{1}{2} =$

2) $3\frac{1}{5} + 2\frac{3}{5} =$

3) $2\frac{2}{7} + 1\frac{1}{7} =$

4) $2\frac{1}{4} + 1\frac{3}{4} =$

5) $2\frac{1}{5} + 4\frac{1}{10} =$

6) $3\frac{2}{5} + 1\frac{3}{5} =$

7) $2\frac{1}{5} + 2\frac{2}{3} =$

8) $3\frac{1}{6} + 5\frac{1}{2} =$

9) $3\frac{3}{7} + 5\frac{4}{7} =$

10) $3 + \frac{1}{3} =$

11) $2\frac{2}{5} + \frac{1}{3} =$

12) $2\frac{1}{3} + 2\frac{1}{9} =$

✎ *Solve.*

13) A baker used $4\frac{1}{2}$ bags of floor baking cakes and $3\frac{3}{5}$ bags of floor baking cookies. How much floor did he used in all?

A. $10\frac{1}{10}$ B. $8\frac{1}{10}$ C. $\frac{16}{10}$ D. $6\frac{2}{10}$

14) Sam bought $2\frac{1}{2}$ kg of sugar from one shop and $6\frac{2}{3}$ kg of sugar from the other shop. How much sugar did he buy in all?

A. $9\frac{1}{6}$ B. $8\frac{1}{6}$ C. $5\frac{1}{6}$ D. $6\frac{1}{6}$

15) A tank has $82\frac{3}{4}$ liters of water. $24\frac{4}{5}$ liters were used and the tank was filled with another $18\frac{3}{4}$ liters. What is the final volume of water in the tank?

A. $75\frac{1}{10}$ B. $70\frac{7}{10}$ C. $76\frac{7}{10}$ D. $76\frac{1}{10}$

Subtract Mixed Numbers

✏️ *Subtract.*

1) $3\frac{2}{3} - 2\frac{1}{3} =$

2) $8\frac{1}{2} - 3\frac{1}{6} =$

3) $6\frac{1}{5} - 3\frac{4}{5} =$

4) $3\frac{1}{7} - 2\frac{2}{7} =$

5) $4\frac{1}{4} - 2\frac{1}{3} =$

6) $5\frac{1}{2} - 3\frac{1}{6} =$

7) $6\frac{1}{4} - 3\frac{1}{2} =$

8) $2\frac{2}{4} - 2\frac{1}{2} =$

9) $2\frac{7}{8} - 3\frac{2}{5} =$

10) $3\frac{1}{3} - 2\frac{2}{6} =$

11) $8\frac{1}{23} - 3\frac{1}{23} =$

12) $3\frac{1}{4} - \frac{7}{12} =$

✏️ *Solve.*

13) When Frodo smiles, his mouth is $2\frac{3}{4}$ in wide. When he is not smiling, his mouth is only $2\frac{1}{4}$ in wide. How much wider is Frodo's mouth when he is smiling than when he is not smiling?

14) Jack jumped $4\frac{1}{7}$ m in a long jump competition. Shane jumped $3\frac{2}{9}$ m. Who jumped longer and by how many meters?

15) Sharon spent $4\frac{3}{7}$ hours studying math and playing tennis. If she played tennis for $2\frac{1}{2}$ hours, how long did she study?

16) Ed just filled up at the gas station, and now his car fuel gauge reads $\frac{8}{10}$ full. He didn't fill the gas tank. If the gauge of fuel was at $\frac{4}{10}$ when he got to the gas station, what fraction of the tank did he fill at the gas station?

Multiplying Mixed Numbers

✎ *Find each product.*

1) $2\frac{3}{4} \times 1\frac{1}{3} =$

2) $2\frac{2}{7} \times 2\frac{4}{5} =$

3) $9\frac{1}{2} \times 3\frac{1}{3} =$

4) $3\frac{1}{5} \times 3\frac{1}{3} =$

5) $4\frac{3}{7} \times 2\frac{5}{8} =$

6) $1\frac{1}{7} \times 2\frac{5}{7} =$

7) $2\frac{1}{2} \times 3\frac{1}{4} =$

8) $1\frac{1}{9} \times 3\frac{1}{2} =$

9) $4\frac{2}{3} \times \frac{3}{7} =$

10) $5\frac{3}{5} \times 2\frac{1}{2} =$

11) $3\frac{1}{5} \times 3\frac{1}{2} =$

12) $4\frac{1}{3} \times 1\frac{1}{3} =$

✎ *Solve.*

13) Kerry read $\frac{2}{3}$ of her chemistry book containing 420 pages. David read $\frac{3}{4}$ of the same. Who read more pages and by how many pages?

14) Victor's weight was 60 kg. He lost $\frac{1}{10}$ of his weight in 3 months. How much weight did he lost?

15) Alex bought 15 kg sweets on his birthday and distributed $\frac{3}{4}$ of it among his friends. How much sweets did he distribute?

16) Shelly distributed a fraction of a cake among 6 girls. Each girl got $\frac{1}{9}$ part of the cake. What fraction of the cake did she distribute in all?

17) The elephants at the Pike Zoo are fed $\frac{1}{2}$ of a barrel of corn each day. The buffalo are fed $\frac{9}{10}$ as much corn as the elephants. How many barrels of corn are the buffalo fed each day?

Dividing Mixed Numbers

✐*Find each quotient.*

1) $3\frac{1}{5} \div 2\frac{2}{3} =$

2) $4\frac{2}{7} \div 3\frac{1}{2} =$

3) $3\frac{1}{3} \div 4\frac{2}{7} =$

4) $3\frac{3}{7} \div 7\frac{1}{3} =$

5) $3\frac{3}{4} \div 1\frac{3}{5} =$

6) $2\frac{7}{8} \div 2\frac{2}{7} =$

7) $1\frac{1}{2} \div 1\frac{2}{5} =$

8) $3\frac{1}{3} \div 2\frac{1}{3} =$

9) $7\frac{1}{7} \div 3\frac{4}{7} =$

10) $3\frac{4}{5} \div 6\frac{1}{3} =$

11) $4\frac{2}{7} \div 7\frac{2}{4} =$

12) $3\frac{1}{5} \div 1\frac{2}{10} =$

13) $1\frac{2}{3} \div 3\frac{1}{3} =$

14) $2\frac{1}{4} \div 1\frac{1}{2} =$

15) $10\frac{1}{2} \div 1\frac{2}{3} =$

16) $3\frac{1}{6} \div 4\frac{2}{3} =$

17) $4\frac{1}{8} \div 2\frac{1}{2} =$

18) $2\frac{1}{10} \div 2\frac{3}{5} =$

19) $1\frac{4}{11} \div 1\frac{1}{4} =$

20) $9\frac{1}{2} \div 9\frac{2}{3} =$

21) $8\frac{3}{4} \div 2\frac{2}{5} =$

22) $12\frac{1}{2} \div 9\frac{1}{3} =$

23) $2\frac{1}{8} \div 1\frac{1}{2} =$

24) $1\frac{1}{10} \div 1\frac{3}{5} =$

✐*Solve.*

25) The product of two numbers is 18. If one number is $8\frac{2}{5}$ find the other number.

26) Ashish cut a 25 m long rope into pieces of $1\frac{2}{3}$ meters each. Find the total number of pieces he cut.

27) The cost of $5\frac{2}{5}$ kg of sugar is $\$101\frac{1}{4}$ find its cost per kg.

28) Ana drinks chocolate milk out of glasses that each hold $\frac{1}{8}$ of a liter. She has $\frac{7}{10}$ of a liter of chocolate milk in her refrigerator. How many glasses of chocolate milk can she pour?

Comparing Decimals

✍ *Write the correct comparison symbol (>, < or =).*

1) 0.632☐0.631

2) 0.75☐1

3) 3.91☐4.91

4) 3.2☐3.1

5) 2.8☐2.801

6) 0.4☐0.74

7) 14.9☐1.49

8) 0.707☐0.0707

9) 1.0001☐0.999

10) 3.655☐6.6555

11) 15.4☐14.5

12) 0.909☐0.99

13) 3.3☐3.33

14) 0.304☐0.304

15) 4.0001☐4.001

16) 3.003☐3.3

17) 2.85☐2.88

18) 0.98☐0.908

19) 2.031☐2.0031

20) 5.97☐5.79

21) 6.302☐6.203

22) 0.075☐0.57

23) 1.04☐1.0401

24) 9.101☐9.011

✍ *Solve.*

25) Write the following decimals in ascending order:

$$5.64, 2.54, 3.05, 0.259 \text{ and } 8.32$$

26) Abril wants a cold drink to take with her to the park. She is choosing between a bottle of sparkling water that contains 502.75 ml and a bottle of plain water that contains 499.793 ml. It is a hot day and Abril wants to bring as much to drink as possible. Which beverage should Abril choose?

Rounding Decimals

✎ *Round each decimal number to the nearest place indicated.*

1) 3.1̲2

2) 0.35̲6

3) 0.4̲9

4) 6̲.75

5) 1.72̲4

6) 3.27̲6

7) 3.3̲45

8) 1̲0̲.66

9) 4̲4̲.93

10) 7.0̲51

11) 12.64̲6

12) 7̲.46

13) 5.8̲63

14) 1̲0̲1̲.03

15) 1̲.53

16) 0.3̲51

17) 1̲0̲0̲.45

18) 7̲.77

✎ *Round off the following to the nearest tenths.*

19) 22.652

20) 30.342

21) 47.847

22) 82.88

23) 16.184

24) 71.79

✎ *Round off the following to the nearest hundredths.*

25) 5.439

26) 12.907

27) 26.1855

28) 48.623

29) 91.448

30) 29.354

✎ *Round off the following to the nearest whole number.*

31) 23.18

32) 8.6

33) 14.45

34) 7.5

35) 3.95

36) 56.7

37) 13.75

38) 12.55

39) 14.25

40) 156

41) 6.52

42) 12.34

43) 50.51

44) 31.501

45) 101.16

Adding and Subtracting Decimals

✎ *Add and subtract decimals.*

1)
$$
\begin{array}{r}
17.81 \\
-\ 10.38 \\
\hline
\end{array}
$$

2)
$$
\begin{array}{r}
37.03 \\
-\ 15.9 \\
\hline
\end{array}
$$

3)
$$
\begin{array}{r}
64.12 \\
-\ 33.33 \\
\hline
\end{array}
$$

4)
$$
\begin{array}{r}
14.58 \\
+15.03 \\
\hline
\end{array}
$$

5)
$$
\begin{array}{r}
17.96 \\
+\ 10.01 \\
\hline
\end{array}
$$

6)
$$
\begin{array}{r}
43.02 \\
+\ 71.08 \\
\hline
\end{array}
$$

7)
$$
\begin{array}{r}
93.09 \\
-\ 66.18 \\
\hline
\end{array}
$$

8)
$$
\begin{array}{r}
76.36 \\
-\ 52.60 \\
\hline
\end{array}
$$

9)
$$
\begin{array}{r}
98.45 \\
+45.56 \\
\hline
\end{array}
$$

10)
$$
\begin{array}{r}
12.5 \\
+11.11 \\
\hline
\end{array}
$$

11)
$$
\begin{array}{r}
34.02 \\
-\ 39.00 \\
\hline
\end{array}
$$

12)
$$
\begin{array}{r}
17.56 \\
+13.98 \\
\hline
\end{array}
$$

✎ *Solve.*

13) $3.56 + \square = 14.7$

14) $\square + 3.5 = 10.6$

15) $12.46 + \square = 17.18$

16) $\square + 6.39 = 10.8$

17) $\square + 3.25 = 5$

18) $14.2 + \square = 17.85$

✎ *Solve.*

19) Henry weighed two colored metal balls during a science class. The yellow ball weighed 0.88 pounds and the green ball weighed 0.47 pounds. If Henry places both balls on the scale at the same time, what will the scale read?

20) Scarlett has a piece of brown ribbon that is 3.41 inches long and a piece of orange ribbon that is 2.22inches long. How much longer is the brown ribbon?

21) Kate had $368.29. Her mother gave her $253.46 and her sister gave her $57.39. How much money does she has now?

Multiplying and Dividing Decimals

✎ *Find each product.*

1)
$$\begin{array}{r} 6.5 \\ \times\, 3.3 \\ \hline \end{array}$$

4)
$$\begin{array}{r} 71.5 \\ \times\, 0.55 \\ \hline \end{array}$$

7)
$$\begin{array}{r} 47.3 \\ \times\, 14.9 \\ \hline \end{array}$$

2)
$$\begin{array}{r} 4.7 \\ \times\, 7.4 \\ \hline \end{array}$$

5)
$$\begin{array}{r} 33.1 \\ \times\, 3.75 \\ \hline \end{array}$$

8)
$$\begin{array}{r} 15.6 \\ \times\, 14.1 \\ \hline \end{array}$$

3)
$$\begin{array}{r} 0.99 \\ \times\, 1.85 \\ \hline \end{array}$$

6)
$$\begin{array}{r} 44.3 \\ \times\, 3.31 \\ \hline \end{array}$$

9)
$$\begin{array}{r} 3.75 \\ \times\, 5.41 \\ \hline \end{array}$$

✎ *Solve.*

10) A hose in a dessert factory pumps out 9.8 liters of chocolate syrup each minute. How many liters of chocolate syrup will the hose pump out in 8 minutes?

11) Diana has a set of wooden boards. Each board is 5.3 meters long. If Diana lays 8 boards end-to-end, how many meters long will the line of boards be?

✎ *Find each quotient.*

12) $19.5 \div 6.2 =$

15) $12.5 \div 3.2 =$

18) $33.8 \div 9.3 =$

13) $45.1 \div 5.5 =$

16) $17.7 \div 10.3 =$

19) $71.1 \div 25.3 =$

14) $35.5 \div 10.5 =$

17) $19.9 \div 20.1 =$

20) $50.3 \div 40.1 =$

✎ *Solve.*

21) A factory used 96.7 kilograms of tomatoes to make 4 batches of pasta sauce. What quantity of tomatoes did the factory put in each batch?

Converting Between Fractions, Decimals and Mixed Numbers

✍️ *Convert fractions to decimals.*

1) $\frac{7}{10} =$ 4) $\frac{3}{8} =$ 7) $\frac{35}{10} =$

2) $\frac{15}{25} =$ 5) $\frac{12}{48} =$ 8) $\frac{75}{15} =$

3) $\frac{6}{18} =$ 6) $\frac{21}{7} =$ 9) $\frac{66}{10} =$

✍️ *Solve.*

10) Maria and Darcy are in the same math class. Maria has completed $\frac{2}{3}$ of her math homework. Darcy has completed $\frac{5}{6}$ of her math homework. Which girl has completed more of her math homework?

11) For track practice, runners were supposed to walk or jog twenty laps. Sara jogged $\frac{3}{4}$ of the laps. Jacob jogged $\frac{3}{5}$ of the laps. Sierra jogged $\frac{1}{2}$ of the laps. List the runners in order from least to greatest number of laps jogged.

12) At a sports banquet, Garrett ate $\frac{5}{6}$ of a pizza. Massey ate $1\frac{1}{3}$ of a pizza. Jaime ate $\frac{1}{2}$ of a pizza. List the students in order from who ate the least to who ate the most.

✍️ *Convert decimal into fraction or mixed numbers.*

13) 0.7   15) 4.3   17) 4.7

14) 0.25   16) 9.25   18) 15.5

Factoring Numbers

✎ List all positive factors of each number.

1) 35

2) 17

3) 42

4) 24

5) 33

6) 22

7) 39

8) 51

9) 34

10) 18

11) 69

12) 58

13) 76

14) 48

15) 14

16) 12

17) 18

18) 20

19) 24

20) 72

21) 85

22) 38

23) 35

24) 8

25) 5

26) 4

27) 36

28) 42

29) 56

30) 63

31) 80

32) 95

33) 102

✎ List the prime factorization for each number.

34) 30

35) 56

36) 78

37) 25

38) 46

39) 28

40) 63

41) 52

42) 18

43) 48

44) 58

45) 36

46) 124

47) 90

48) 69

49) 72

50) 85

51) 21

52) 12

53) 18

54) 24

55) 55

56) 75

57) 9

58) 10

59) 15

60) 14

Greatest Common Factor

✎ *Find the GCF for each number pair.*

1) 36,12	6) 14,42	11) 17,34
2) 18,34	7) 15,80	12) 54,14
3) 25,55	8) 10,35	13) 39,24
4) 18,48	9) 70,30	14) 30,65
5) 21,90	10) 28,36	15) 72,20

✎ *Solve.*

16) Sara has 16 red flowers and 24 yellow flowers. She wants to make a bouquet with the same of each color flower in each bouquet. What is the greatest number of bouquets she can make?

17) At a concert, the band has 8 men's T-shirts and 16 women's T-shirts. The band wants to set up tables to sell the shirts, with an equal number of men's and women's shirts available at each table and no shirts left over. What is the greatest number of tables the band can sell shirts from?

18) Nancy is planting 6 bushes and 15 trees in rows. If she wants all the rows to be the same, with no plants left over, what is the greatest number of rows Nancy can plant?

19) Peter has 12 dollars in his pocket and James has 15 dollars. They want to give money to each other. How much money will they have left after they give to each other the same but highest possible amount?

Least Common Multiple

🖎 Find the LCM for each number pair.

1) 25,10

2) 36,18

3) 8,10

4) 12,18

5) 24,32

6) 14,10

7) 8,28

8) 51,57

9) 20,15,10

10) 12,20,28

11) 15,75

12) 10,25

13) 9,7

14) 78,6

15) 22,10,2

16) 12,4,16

17) 9,21

18) 25,15,20

19) 70,10

20) 12,18,24

21) 15,45,30

🖎 Solve.

22) Becky is packing equal quantities of pretzels and crackers for snacks. Becky bags the pretzels in groups of 4 and the crackers in groups of 18. What is the smallest number of crackers that she can pack?

23) Sam and Carlos are bowling with plastic pins in Sam's living room. Remarkably, Sam knocks down 8 pins on every bowl, and Carlos knocks down 9 pins on every bowl. At the end of the day, Sam and Carlos have knocked down the same total number of pins. What is the least number of total pins that Sam and Carlos could have each knocked down?

24) Regan's Bakery sells muffins in packages of 9 and cookies in packages of 11. Going through yesterday's receipts, a store manager notices that the bakery sold the same number of muffins and cookies yesterday afternoon. What is the smallest number of muffins that the bakery could have sold?

Answers of Worksheets

Simplifying Fractions

1) $\frac{11}{18}$
2) $\frac{4}{5}$
3) $\frac{2}{3}$
4) $\frac{3}{4}$
5) $\frac{1}{3}$
6) $\frac{1}{4}$

7) $\frac{4}{9}$
8) $\frac{1}{2}$
9) $\frac{2}{5}$
10) $\frac{1}{9}$
11) $\frac{5}{9}$
12) $\frac{3}{4}$

13) $\frac{5}{8}$
14) $\frac{13}{16}$
15) $\frac{1}{5}$
16) $\frac{4}{7}$
17) $\frac{1}{2}$
18) $\frac{5}{12}$

19) $\frac{3}{8}$
20) $\frac{1}{4}$
21) $\frac{5}{9}$
22) B
23) A
24) C

Adding and Subtracting Fractions

1) $\frac{11}{10}$
2) $\frac{31}{35}$
3) $\frac{15}{28}$
4) $\frac{61}{24}$
5) $\frac{7}{10}$
6) $\frac{8}{9}$

7) $\frac{11}{14}$
8) $\frac{19}{12}$
9) $\frac{18}{21}$
10) $\frac{2}{5}$
11) $\frac{3}{10}$
12) $\frac{1}{6}$

13) $\frac{17}{40}$
14) $\frac{1}{5}$
15) $\frac{3}{10}$
16) $\frac{7}{18}$
17) $-\frac{1}{3}$
18) $\frac{3}{40}$

19) $\frac{1}{2}$
20) $5\frac{2}{3}$
21) $\frac{3}{8}$

Multiplying and Dividing Fractions

1) $\frac{10}{63}$
2) $\frac{3}{14}$
3) $\frac{2}{7}$
4) $\frac{2}{15}$
5) $\frac{3}{5}$
6) $\frac{45}{77}$

7) $\frac{2}{9}$
8) $\frac{3}{10}$
9) $\frac{4}{9}$
10) $\frac{5}{27}$
11) $\frac{7}{12}$
12) $\frac{6}{7}$

13) $\frac{32}{39}$
14) $\frac{3}{10}$
15) $\frac{2}{15}$
16) $\frac{4}{3}$
17) $\frac{11}{2}$
18) $\frac{3}{2}$

19) 5
20) 6
21) 4
22) $\frac{18}{5}$
23) 2

Adding Mixed Numbers

1) $3\frac{3}{4}$

2) $5\frac{4}{5}$

3) $3\frac{3}{7}$

4) 4

5) $6\frac{3}{10}$

6) 5

7) $4\frac{13}{15}$

8) $8\frac{2}{3}$

9) 9

10) $3\frac{1}{3}$

11) $2\frac{11}{15}$

12) $4\frac{4}{9}$

13) $8\frac{1}{10}$

14) $9\frac{1}{6}$

15) $76\frac{7}{10}$

Subtract Mixed Numbers

1) $1\frac{1}{3}$

2) $5\frac{1}{3}$

3) $2\frac{2}{5}$

4) $\frac{6}{7}$

5) $1\frac{11}{12}$

6) $2\frac{1}{3}$

7) $2\frac{3}{4}$

8) 0

9) $-\frac{21}{40}$

10) 1

11) 5

12) $2\frac{2}{3}$

13) $\frac{1}{2}$

14) $\frac{58}{63}$, Jack

15) $1\frac{13}{14}$

16) $\frac{2}{5}$

Multiplying Mixed Numbers

1) $3\frac{2}{3}$

2) $6\frac{2}{5}$

3) $31\frac{2}{3}$

4) $10\frac{2}{3}$

5) $11\frac{5}{8}$

6) $21\frac{5}{7}$

7) $8\frac{1}{8}$

8) $3\frac{8}{9}$

9) 2

10) 14

11) $11\frac{1}{5}$

12) $5\frac{7}{9}$

13) David, 315 pages

14) 6kg

15) $11\frac{1}{4}$

16) $\frac{6}{9}$

17) $\frac{9}{20}$

Dividing Mixed Numbers

1) $1\frac{1}{5}$

2) $1\frac{11}{49}$

3) $\frac{7}{9}$

4) $\frac{36}{77}$

5) $2\frac{11}{32}$

6) $1\frac{33}{128}$

7) $1\frac{1}{14}$

8) $1\frac{3}{7}$

9) 2

10) $\frac{3}{5}$

11) $\frac{4}{7}$

12) $2\frac{2}{3}$

13) $\frac{1}{2}$

14) $1\frac{1}{2}$

15) $6\frac{3}{10}$

16) $\frac{19}{28}$

17) $1\frac{13}{20}$

18) $\frac{21}{26}$

19) $1\frac{1}{11}$

20) $\frac{57}{58}$

21) $3\frac{31}{48}$

22) $1\frac{19}{56}$

23) $1\frac{5}{12}$

24) $\frac{11}{16}$

25) $2\frac{1}{7}$

26) 15

27) $18\frac{3}{4}$

28) $5\frac{3}{5}$

Comparing Decimals

1) $0.632 > 0.631$

2) $0.75 < 1$

3) $3.91 < 4.91$

4) $3.2 > 3.1$

5) $2.8 < 2.801$

6) $0.47 < 0.74$

7) $14.9 > 1.49$

8) $0.707 > 0.0707$

9) $1.01 > 0.999$

10) $3.655 < 6.6555$

11) $15.4 > 14.5$

12) $0.909 < 0.99$

13) $3.3 < 3.33$

14) $0.304 = 0.304$

15) $4.0001 < 4.001$

16) $3.003 < 3.3$

17) $2.85 < 2.88$

18) $0.98 > 0.908$

19) $2.031 > 2.0031$

20) $5.97 > 5.79$

21) $6.302 > 6.203$

22) $0.075 < 0.57$

23) $1.04 < 1.0401$

24) $9.101 > 9.011$

25) $0.259, 2.54, 3.05, 5.46, 8.32$

26) sparkling water

Rounding Decimals

1) 3.1

2) 0.36

3) 0.5

4) 7

5) 1.72

6) 3.28

7) 3.3

8) 11

9) 45

10) 7.1

11) 12.65

12) 7

13) 5.9

14) 101

15) 2

16) 0.4

17) 100

18) 8

19) 22.7

20) 30.3

21) 47.9

22) 82.9

23) 16.2

24) 71.8

25) 5.44

26) 12.91

27) 26.19

28) 48.62

29) 91.45

30) 29.35

31) 23

32) 9

33) 14

34) 8

35) 4

36) 57

37) 14

38) 13

39) 14

40) 156

41) 7

42) 12

43) 51

44) 32

45) 101

Adding and Subtracting Decimals

1) 7.43

2) 21.13

3) 30.79

4) 29.61

5) 27.97

6) 114.1

7) 26.91

8) 23.76

9) 144.01

10) 23.61

11) -4.98

12) 31.54

13) 11.14

14) 7.1

15) 4.72

16) 4.41

17) 1.75

18) 3.65

19) 1.35

20) 1.19

21) $679.14

Multiplying and Dividing Decimals

1) 21.45
2) 34.78
3) 1.8315
4) 39.325
5) 124.125
6) 146.633
7) 704.77
8) 219.96
9) 20.2875
10) 78.4
11) 42.4
12) 3.14
13) 8.2
14) 3.38
15) 3.9
16) 1.71
17) 0.99
18) 3.63
19) 2.81
20) 1.25
21) 24.175

Converting Between Fractions, Decimals and Mixed Numbers

1) 0.7
2) 0.6
3) 0.33
4) 0.375
5) 0.25
6) 3
7) 3.5
8) 5
9) 6.6
10) Darcy, 0.833 …
11) Sierra(0.5), Jacob(0.6), Sara(0.75)
12) James(0.5), Garret(0.833), Massey(1.33)
13) $\frac{7}{10}$
14) $\frac{1}{4}$
15) $4\frac{3}{10}$
16) $9\frac{25}{100}$
17) $4\frac{7}{10}$
18) $15\frac{5}{10}$

Factoring Numbers

1) 1,5,7,35
2) 1,17
3) 1,2,3,6,7,14,21,42
4) 1,2,3,4,6,8,12,24
5) 1,3,11,33
6) 1,2,11,22
7) 1,3,13,39
8) 1,3,17,51
9) 1,2,17,34
10) 1,2,3,6,9,18
11) 1,3,23,69
12) 1,2,29,58
13) 1,2,4,19,38,76
14) 1,2,3,4,6,8,12,16,24,48
15) 1,2,7,14
16) 1,2,3,4,6,12
17) 1,2,3,4,6,9,18
18) 1,2,4,5,10,20
19) 1,2,3,4,6,8,12,24
20) 1,2,3,4,6,8,12,18,24,36,72
21) 1,5,17,85

22) 1,2,19,38

23) 1,5,7,35

24) 1,2,4,8

25) 1,5

26) 1,2,4

27) 1,2,3,4,6,9,12,18,36

28) 1,2,3,6,7,14,21,42

29) 1,2,4,7,8,14,28,56

30) 1,3,7,9,21,63

31) 1,2,4,5,8,10,16,20,40,80

32) 1,5,19,95

33) 1,2,3,6,17,34,51,102

34) $2 \times 3 \times 5$

35) $2 \times 2 \times 2 \times 7$

36) $2 \times 3 \times 13$

37) 5×5

38) 2×23

39) $2 \times 2 \times 7$

40) $3 \times 3 \times 7$

41) $2 \times 2 \times 13$

42) $2 \times 3 \times 3$

43) $2 \times 2 \times 2 \times 2 \times 3$

44) 2×29

45) $2 \times 2 \times 3 \times 3$

46) $2 \times 2 \times 31$

47) $2 \times 5 \times 9$

48) 3×23

49) $2 \times 2 \times 2 \times 3 \times 3$

50) 5×17

51) 3×7

52) $2 \times 3 \times 4$

53) $2 \times 3 \times 3$

54) $2 \times 2 \times 2 \times 3$

55) 5×11

56) $3 \times 5 \times 5$

57) 3×3

58) 2×5

59) 3×5

60) 2×7

61) $2 \times 3 \times 3$

62) 19

63) $2 \times 2 \times 5$

Greatest Common Factor

1) 12

2) 2

3) 5

4) 6

5) 3

6) 14

7) 5

8) 5

9) 10

10) 4

11) 17

12) 2

13) 3

14) 5

15) 4

16) 8

17) 8

18) 3

19) 3

Least Common Multiple

1) 50

2) 36

3) 40

4) 36

5) 96

6) 70

7) 56

8) 969

9) 60

10) 420

11) 75

12) 50

13) 63

14) 78

15) 110

16) 48

17) 63

18) 300

19) 70

20) 72

21) 90

22) 36

23) 72

24) 99

Chapter 2:

Real Numbers and Integers

Topics that you'll learn in this part:

- ✓ Adding and Subtracting Integers
- ✓ Multiplying and Dividing Integers
- ✓ Ordering Integers and Numbers
- ✓ Arrange and Order, Comparing Integers
- ✓ Order of Operations
- ✓ Mixed Integer Computations
- ✓ Integers and Absolute Value

Adding and Subtracting Integers

✍ *Find the sum.*

1) $(-37) + (-8) =$

2) $8 + (-17) =$

3) $(-53) + (-7) =$

4) $(-41) + (23) =$

5) $(-14) + (-5) =$

6) $(-72) + (-30) + 2 =$

7) $4 + (-40) + (-15) + (-21) =$

8) $91 + (-143) + (-45) =$

9) $(-33) + (-18) =$

10) $(-14) + (58 - 44) =$

✍ *Find the difference.*

11) $(-34) - (-28) - 4 =$

12) $54 - (-12) =$

13) $(-35) - (-5) =$

14) $(-51) - (-34) =$

15) $(-45) - (-30) =$

16) $(-15) - (-10) =$

17) $(-30) - (-14) - (-17) =$

18) $(-10) - (-10) - (-3) =$

19) $(-45) - (-17) =$

20) $(-7) - (-34) - 17 =$

✍ *Solve.*

21) The leaderboard at the Stamford Golf Tournament shows that Nancy's score is 5 and Doug's score is (-1). How many more strokes did Nancy take than Doug?

22) Bridget carefully tracks her money. Her records indicate she spent $300 on a hammock and deposited $1,000 she made from an online auction. Which integer represents the change in how much money Bridget had?

Multiplying and Dividing Integers

✍️*Find each product.*

1) $(-11) \times (-5) =$

2) $34 \times (-2) =$

3) $(-4) \times 5 =$

4) $7 \times (-10) =$

5) $(-11) \times (-2) \times 2 =$

6) $6 \times (-1\,5) =$

7) $14 \times (-14) =$

8) $(-13) \times (-10) =$

9) $(-14) \times (-4) \times (-5) =$

10) $14 \times (-5) =$

✍️*Find each quotient.*

11) $210 \div (-14) =$

12) $(-208) \div (-13) =$

13) $(108) \div (-9) =$

14) $(-161) \div (-23) =$

15) $84 \div (-14) =$

16) $(-484) \div (-22) =$

17) $(-162) \div (-18) =$

18) $198 \div 6 =$

✍️*Solve.*

19) Adam is scuba diving. He descends 5 feet. He descends the same distance 4 more times. What integer represents Adam's new DISTANCE from sea level?

20) The price of jeans was reduced $6 per week for 7 weeks. By how much did the price of the jeans change over the 7 weeks?

21) Yesterday's low temperature was (-2°C). Today's low temperature is 3 times as low as yesterday's low temperature. What is today's low temperature?

Ordering Integers and Numbers

✍ *Order each set of integers from least to greatest.*

1) $36, -10, 0, 17, 2, -12$ ___, ___, ___, ___, ___, ___

2) $43, 10, 21, -30, -1, -12, 2$ ___, ___, ___, ___, ___, ___

3) $45, -10, 14, -14, 0, -3$ ___, ___, ___, ___, ___, ___

4) $-100, 0, 100, 10$ ___, ___, ___, ___, ___, ___

5) $56, -2, -3, -50$ ___, ___, ___, ___, ___, ___

6) $18, -6, 15, -1, -10$ ___, ___, ___, ___, ___, ___

7) $-20, 12, 0, 15, -30, -2$ ___, ___, ___, ___, ___, ___

8) $50, 12, -52, -12, -3$ ___, ___, ___, ___, ___, ___

9) $-9, -1, 0, 2, 3, -6$ ___, ___, ___, ___, ___, ___

10) $12, 21, -14, 8, -9, 10$ ___, ___, ___, ___, ___, ___

✍ *Order each set of integers from greatest to least.*

11) $-99, 7, 10, 0$ ___, ___, ___, ___, ___, ___

12) $5, -4, -2, 0, 10$ ___, ___, ___, ___, ___, ___

13) $-30, -100, 33, -33$ ___, ___, ___, ___, ___, ___

14) $-81, 10, 71, 23, 51, 12, -3$ ___, ___, ___, ___, ___, ___

15) $-3, -2, 6, -32, 5, 12$ ___, ___, ___, ___, ___, ___

16) $13, -1, 1, 0, -13$ ___, ___, ___, ___, ___, ___

17) $79, 0, 12, -100$ ___, ___, ___, ___, ___, ___

18) $99, -1, 23, -3, 0$ ___, ___, ___, ___, ___, ___

19) $44, -6, -100, 19$ ___, ___, ___, ___, ___, ___

Arrange, Order, and Comparing Integers

✍ *Arrange these integers in descending order.*

1) $34, 15, -3, -4$

____, ____, ____, ____, ____, ____

2) $17, -10, 0, -14$

____, ____, ____, ____, ____, ____

3) $15, -78, -15, -1$

____, ____, ____, ____, ____, ____

4) $35, -17, 12, -45$

____, ____, ____, ____, ____, ____

5) $-30, -10, 71, -15, -14$

____, ____, ____, ____, ____, ____

6) $62, -20, 12, 15, 14, 0$

____, ____, ____, ____, ____, ____

7) $-369, 12, -1, 1, 0, -95$

____, ____, ____, ____, ____, ____

8) $62, -41, -1, 3, 14, 7, -7$

____, ____, ____, ____, ____, ____

9) $36, -100, 100, -5, 5$

____, ____, ____, ____, ____, ____

10) $99, -87, 56, -45, -110$

____, ____, ____, ____, ____, ____

✍ *Compare. Use >, =, <*

11) $-15 \,\square\, 12 =$

12) $-33 \,\square\, -16 =$

13) $-65 \,\square\, 0 =$

14) $30 \quad -35 =$

15) $96 \quad -96 =$

16) $-568 \,\square\, -658 =$

17) $-321 \,\square\, -321 =$

18) $545 \,\square\, -545 =$

19) $-1000 \,\square\, -965 =$

20) $-25 \,\square\, -656 =$

21) $-89 \,\square\, -100 =$

22) $0 \,\square\, -1 =$

23) $10 \,\square\, -11 =$

24) $79 \,\square\, -100 =$

25) $95 \quad 89 =$

26) $0.2 \,\square\, -0.2 =$

27) $12 \,\square\, -15 =$

28) $9 \,\square\, -9 =$

Order of Operations

✎ *Evaluate each expression.*

1) $15 + \left(\dfrac{66}{12-((-5)\times 2)}\right) =$

2) $\dfrac{(-55)}{5} + 10 =$

3) $(-13) + (6 \div 2) =$

4) $\dfrac{45}{(-15)} + (3 \times 2) =$

5) $(-40) + \left(6 \times (-7)\right) =$

6) $\left(5 \times (-7)\right) - \dfrac{40}{8} =$

7) $(-78) - \dfrac{28}{(-2)} =$

8) $\dfrac{(-80)}{(-4)} =$

9) $15 - \left(3 \times (-7)\right) =$

10) $45 + \left(3 \times (-15)\right) =$

11) $45 - \left(\dfrac{3 \times 10}{4+(-2)}\right) =$

12) $(-48) - \dfrac{8}{2} =$

13) $\dfrac{(-35)}{7} + 3 =$

14) $\left(\dfrac{70}{(-14)}\right) - (2 \times 3) =$

15) $36 + \left((-2) \times 3\right) =$

16) $15 - \dfrac{30}{(-6)} =$

17) $78 + (-13) =$

18) $6 + \dfrac{(-51)}{(-17)} =$

19) $5 - \dfrac{25}{-10} =$

20) $\dfrac{3(15-8)}{7} + 5 =$

21) $\left(\dfrac{25-13}{2(3)} - 7\right) \times 2 =$

22) $5 \times \left(\dfrac{55}{11}\right) + 8 =$

23) $(-12) \times \dfrac{48}{6} + 12 =$

24) $\dfrac{96}{-12} - 6 =$

25) $\dfrac{(33 \times 2)}{(-6) \times 11} + 1 =$

26) $12 \times \left(\dfrac{45}{(-5)}\right) =$

✎ *Solve.*

27) Sylvia bought 6 bananas for 60 cents each and 1 apple for 90 cents. Write a numerical expression to represent this situation and then find the total cost in dollar.

Mixed Integer Computations

✍ *Compute.*

1) $(-70) \div \left(\frac{20}{4}\right) =$

2) $(-21) \times \frac{(-3)}{7} =$

3) $(-10) \times \left(-\frac{14}{5}\right) =$

4) $\left(\frac{3+(-13)}{2}\right) \div 5 =$

5) $18 \times \frac{24}{(-18)} =$

6) $(-90) \div \frac{(-45)}{14} =$

7) $\frac{\left(-\frac{48}{4}\right)}{\left(\frac{60}{30}\right)} \times \frac{25}{(-5)} =$

8) $\left(2 \times \frac{24}{(-4)}\right) \div (-6) =$

9) $78 \div (-6) =$

10) $\frac{(-27)}{3} \times \left(-\frac{14}{7}\right) =$

11) $5 \times \left((-4) + \frac{15}{5}\right) =$

12) $\frac{(-48)}{4} \div (-2) =$

13) $\frac{(-36)}{12} \times (-2) =$

14) $(-10) \times (9) =$

15) $\frac{30}{(-6)} \times \frac{(-45)}{(-15)} =$

16) $(-100) \div \left(\frac{(-100)}{45}\right) =$

17) $(-80) \div (-20) =$

18) $(-6) \times (-11) =$

19) $(-3) \times \frac{(14 \times (-3))}{42} =$

20) $2 \times \left(-\frac{56}{8}\right) =$

21) $\frac{5}{2} \div \frac{10}{6} =$

22) $(-24) \div \frac{24}{10} + 5 =$

23) $\frac{25}{(-5)} \div \frac{1}{5} =$

24) $\frac{72 \div 12}{35 \div 5} \times 7 =$

25) $\frac{3(50 \div 5)}{30} \div \frac{10}{45} =$

26) $\frac{25}{5} \div \frac{25}{125} =$

27) $\frac{56}{7} \times \left(3 - \frac{42}{7}\right) =$

28) $3 \times \frac{24}{6} + 5 =$

29) $\frac{3}{10} \times \frac{-10}{7} =$

30) $\frac{(-25)}{11} \div \frac{40}{11} =$

31) $45 \div \left(\frac{4}{3} \div \frac{8}{6}\right) =$

32) $(-3) \div \left(\frac{(-20)}{66}\right) =$

33) $\left(\frac{45}{20}\right) \times \left(\frac{15}{20} \div \frac{10}{12}\right) =$

34) $\frac{1}{2} \times \left(3 - \frac{1}{3}\right) =$

Integers and Absolute Value

✍ *Write absolute value of each number.*

1) -78

2) -1

3) -65

4) 56

5) -98

6) -11

7) -21

8) 3

9) 2

10) -42

11) -61

12) -10

13) 36

14) -13

15) -33

16) -22

17) -19

18) 17

19) -14

20) -41

21) -98

✍ *Evaluate.*

22) $|-22| - |12| =$

23) $12 + |-15 - 10| - |-3| =$

24) $|-16| - 40 + 30 =$

25) $|-113| - |(-35) + 30| =$

26) $|12 - 4| + 6 - |-9| =$

27) $|-52| + |-10| =$

28) $|-2 + 8| + |7 - 7| =$

29) $|-12| + |-11| =$

✍ *Solve.*

30) You have money in your wallet, but you don't know the exact amount. When a friend asks you, you say that you have 50 dollars give or take 15. Use an absolute value equation to find least and biggest amount of money in your pocket?

31) The ideal selling price of a Toyota is 25000. The dealer allows this price to vary 5%. What is the lowest price this dealer can sell this Toyota?

Answers of Worksheets

Adding and Subtracting Integers

1) −45	7) −72	13) −30	19) −28
2) −9	8) −97	14) −17	20) 10
3) −60	9) −51	15) −15	21) 6
4) −18	10) 0	16) −5	22) 700
5) −19	11) −10	17) 1	
6) −100	12) 66	18) 3	

Multiplying and Dividing Integers

1) 55	7) −196	13) −12	19) −25
2) −68	8) 130	14) 7	20) −42
3) −20	9) −280	15) −6	21) −6
4) −70	10) −70	16) 22	
5) 44	11) −15	17) 9	
6) −90	12) 16	18) 33	

Ordering Integers and Numbers

1) −12, −10, 0, 2, 17, 36	8) −52, −12, −3, 12, 50	15) 12, 6, 5, −2, −3, −32
2) −30, −12, −1, 2, 10, 21, 43	9) −9, −6, −1, 0, 2, 3	16) 13, 1, 0, −1, −13
3) −14, −10, −3, 0, 14, 45	10) −14, −9, 10, 12, 21	17) 79, 12, 0, −100
4) −100, 0, 10, 100	11) 10, 7, 0, −99	18) 99, 23, 0, −1, −3
5) −50, −3, −2, 56	12) 10.5, 0, −2, −4	19) 44, 19, −6, −100
6) −10, −6, −1, 15, 18	13) 33, −30, −33, −100	
7) −30, −20, −2, 0, 12, 15	14) 71, 51, 23, 12, 10, −3, −81	

Arrange and Order, Comparing Integers

1) 34, 15, −3, −4	5) 71, −10, −14, −15, −30	9) 100, 36, 5, −5, −100
2) 17, 0, −10, −14	6) 62, 15, 14, 12, 0, −20	10) 99, 56, −45, −87, −110
3) 15, −1, −15, −78	7) 12, 1, 0, −1, −95, −369	11) <
4) 35, 12, −17, −45	8) 62, 14, 7, 3, −1, −7, −41	12) <

13) <   19) <   25) >

14) >   20) >   26) >

15) >   21) >   27) >

16) >   22) >   28) >

17) =   23) >

18) >   24) >

Order of Operations

1) 18   8) 20   15) 30   22) 33

2) −1   9) 36   16) 20   23) −84

3) −10   10) 0   17) 65   24) −14

4) 3   11) 30   18) 9   25) 0

5) −82   12) −52   19) 7.5   26) −108

6) −40   13) −2   20) 8   27) $4.5

7) −64   14) −11   21) −10

Mixed Integer Computations

1) −14   10) 18   19) 3   28) 17

2) 9   11) −5   20) −14   29) $-\frac{3}{7}$

3) 28   12) 6   21) $\frac{3}{2}$ 30) $\frac{(-25)}{40}$

4) −1   13) 6   22) −5   31) 45

5) −24   14) −90   23) −25   32) $\frac{99}{10}$

6) 28   15) −15   24) 6   33) $\frac{81}{40}$

7) 30   16) 45   25) 4.5

8) 2   17) 4   26) 25   34) $\frac{8}{6}$

9) −13   18) 66   27) −24

Integers and Absolute Value

1) 78   3) 65   5) 98   7) 21

2) 1   4) 56   6) 11   8) 3

9) 2	15) 33	21) 98	27) 62
10) 42	16) 22	22) 10	28) 6
11) 61	17) 19	23) 34	29) 23
12) 10	18) 17	24) 6	30) 35,65
13) 36	19) 14	25) 108	31) 23750
14) 13	20) 41	26) 5	

Chapter 3:

Proportions and Ratios

Math Topics that you'll learn in this part:

- ✓ Writing Ratios
- ✓ Simplifying Ratios
- ✓ Proportional Ratios
- ✓ Create a Proportion
- ✓ Similar Figures
- ✓ Similar Figure Word Problems
- ✓ Ratio and Rates Word Problems

Writing Ratios

✍ ***Express each ratio as a rate and unite rate.***

1) 150 miles on 5 gallons of gas.

2) 20 dollars for 4 books.

3) 100 miles on 8 gallons of gas

4) 30 inches of snow in 10 hours

✍ ***Express each ratio as a fraction in the simplest form.***

5) 6 feet out of 24 feet

6) 12 cakes out of 24 cakes

7) 7 dimes of 35 dimes

8) 16 dimes out of 48 coins

9) 21 cups to 56 cups

10) 36 gallons to 85 gallons

11) 18 miles out of 42 miles

12) 23 blue cars out of 46 cars

✍ ***Solve.***

13) In a telephone poll, 10 people said they like shopping and 20 people said they do not like shopping. What is the ratio of the number of people who do not like shopping to the number of people who like shopping?

14) There are 30 pink beads and 6 purple beads on Maria's necklace. What is the ratio of the number of pink beads to the number of purple beads?

15) 40 of the tables at Gary's Italian Restaurant are full and the other 8 tables are empty. What is the ratio of the number of full tables to the number of empty tables?

Simplifying Ratios

🖎*Reduce each ratio.*

1) 42 : 70

2) 18 : 54

3) 15 : 45

4) 21 : 45

5) 10 : 60

6) 46 : 92

7) 50 : 20

8) 12 : 40

9) 90 : 45

10) 20 : 85

11) 28 : 40

12) 12 : 72

13) 24 : 12

14) 55 : 25

15) 39 : 13

16) 14 : 77

17) 18 : 66

18) 8 : 32

19) 45 : 100

20) 6 : 30

21) 17 : 85

22) 36 : 90

23) 15 : 80

24) 40 : 100

🖎 *Each pair of figures is similar. Find the missing side.*

25)

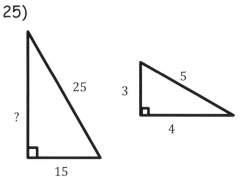

26)

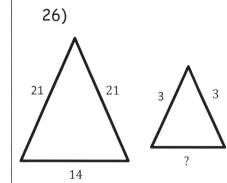

27)

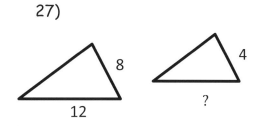

28)

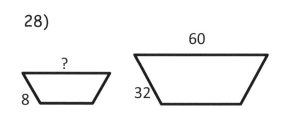

Create a Proportion

🖎 *Create proportion from the given set of numbers.*

1) $1, 15, 5, 3$

2) $12, 36, 4, 12$

3) $32, 8, 8, 2$

4) $17, 5, 51, 15$

5) $9, 7, 54, 42$

6) $56, 5, 8, 35$

7) $3, 5, 55, 33$

8) $12, 12, 3, 48$

🖎 *Solve.*

9) In a party, 10 soft drinks are required for every 12 guests. If there are 252 guests, how many soft drinks is required?

10) Mika can eat 21 hot dogs in 6 minutes. She wants to know how many minutes (m) it would take her to eat 35 hot dogs if she can keep up the same pace.

11) Mandy works construction. She knows that a 5-meter-long metal bar has a mass of 40kg. Mandy wants to figure out the mass (w) of a bar made of the same metal that is 3 meters long and the same thickness. What is the mass of the shorter bar?

12) Kwesi is putting on sunscreen. He uses 3ml to cover 45cm² of his skin. He wants to know how many milliliters of sunscreen (g) he needs to cover 240cm² of his skin. He assumes the relationship between milliliters of sunscreen and area is proportional. How many milliliters of sunscreen does Kwesi need to cover 240cm² of his skin?

Similar Figures

✎ *Each pair of figures is similar. Find the missing side.*

1)

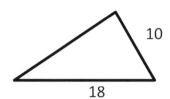

2)

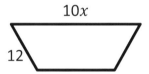

3)

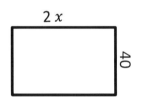

4)

5)

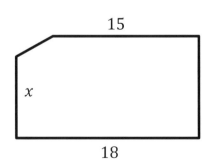

Simple Interest

🖎*Use simple interest to find the ending balance.*

1) $1,200 at 3% for 5 years.

2) $5,650 at 6% for 4 months.

3) $1600 at 8% for 8 years

4) $12,000 at 6.5% for 6 years.

5) $3200 at 4% for 7 years.

6) $32,500 at 8% for 6 years.

🖎*Solve.*

7) $300 interest is earned on a principal of $2000 at a simple interest rate of 5% interest per year. For how many years was the principal invested?

8) A new car, valued at $30,000, depreciates at 8% per year from original price. Find the value of the car 2 years after purchase.

9) Sara puts $4,000 into an investment yielding 7% annual simple interest; she left the money in for four years. How much interest does Sara get at the end of those four years?

10) You want to save $1,200 to buy your first self-driving magic carpet. You deposit $8,000 in a bank at an interest rate of 5% per annum. How many years do you have to wait before you can buy your magic carpet?

11) Aladdin has 12 extra gold coins in his magic bag. The Genie tells him that for every 100 gold coins he has in his magic bag, he will get 25 extra gold coins every year. How many years later will Aladdin have 21 gold coins in his bag?

Ratio and Rates Word Problems

📝 *Solve.*

1) In a party, 10 soft drinks are required for every 14 guests. If there are 266 guests, how many soft drinks is required?

2) In Jack's class, 12 of the students are tall and 8 are short. In Michael's class 26 students are tall and 14 students are short. Which class has a higher ratio of tall to short students?

3) Are these ratios equivalent? 13 cards to 78 animals 15marbles to 90 marbles.

4) The price of 4 apples at the Quick Market is$3. The price of 7 of the same apples at Walmart is $5.50. Which place is the better buy?

5) The bakers at a Bakery can make 200 bagels in 5 hours. How many bagels can they bake in 15 hours? What is that rate per hour?

6) You can buy 8 cans of green beans at a supermarket for $5.20. How much does it cost to buy 45 cans of green beans?

7) Finley makes 11 batch of her favorite shade of orange paint by mixing 55 liters of yellow paint with 33 liters of red paint. How many batches of orange paint can Finley make if she has 15 liters of red paint?

8) Quinn is playing video games at a virtual reality game room. The game room charges 20 dollars for every 30 minutes of play time. How much does Quinn need to pay for 150 minutes of play time.

Answers of Worksheets

Writing Ratios

1) $\frac{150\ miles}{5\ gallons}$, 30 miles per gallon

2) $\frac{20\ dollars}{4\ books}$, 5.00 dollars per book

3) $\frac{100\ miles}{8\ gallons}$, 12.5 miles per gallon

4) $\frac{30"\ of\ snow}{10\ hours}$, 3 inches of snow per hour

5) $\frac{1}{4}$	7) $\frac{1}{5}$	9) $\frac{3}{8}$	11) $\frac{3}{7}$	14) 5
6) $\frac{1}{2}$	8) $\frac{1}{3}$	10) $\frac{36}{85}$	12) $\frac{1}{2}$	15) 5
			13) 2	

Simplifying Ratios

1) 3:5	7) 5:2	13) 2:1	19) 9:20	25) 20
2) 1:3	8) 3:10	14) 11:5	20) 1:5	26) 2
3) 1:3	9) 2:1	15) 3:1	21) 1:6	27) 6
4) 7:15	10) 4:17	16) 2:11	22) 2:5	28) 15
5) 1:6	11) 7:10	17) 3:11	23) 3:16	
6) 1:2	12) 1:6	18) 1:4	24) 2:5	

Create a Proportion

1) $1:3 = 5:15$	5) $7:42 = 9:54$	9) 210
2) $12:36 = 4:12$	6) $5:35 = 8:56$	10) 10
3) $2:8 = 8:32$	7) $3:33 = 5:55$	11) 24
4) $5:15 = 17:51$	8) $3:12 = 12:48$	12) 16

Similar Figures

1) 9	2) 3	3) 24	4) 15	5) 6

Simple Interest

1) $1380.00	4) $16,680.00	7) 3 years	9) $1,120
2) $7,006.00	5) $4,096.00	8) $25,200	10) 3 years
3) $2,624.00	6) $48,100.00		

11) %5

Ratio and Rates Word Problems

1) 190

2) The ratio for Michael's class is higher and equal to 13 to 7.

3) Yes! Both ratios are 1 to 6

4) The price at the Quick Market is a better buy.

5) 600, the rate is 40 per hour.

6) $29.25

7) 5

8) 100

Chapter 4:

Percent

Math Topics that you'll learn in this part:

- ✓ Percentage Calculations
- ✓ Converting Between Percent, Fractions, and Decimals
- ✓ Percent Problems
- ✓ Find What Percentage a Number Is of Another
- ✓ Find a Percentage of a Given Number
- ✓ Percent of Increase and Decrease
- ✓ Markup, Discount, and Tax

Percentage Calculations

✏ *Calculate the percentages.*

1) 10% of 50 =

2) 15% of 80 =

3) 50% of 26 =

4) 30% of 20 =

5) 45% of 100 =

6) 25% of 100 =

7) 70% of 30 =

8) 38% of 50 =

9) 20% of 50 =

10) 75% of 100 =

11) 65% of 80 =

12) 30% of 50 =

13) 20% of 0 =

14) 84% of 200 =

15) 12% of 100 =

16) 40% of 300 =

17) 30% of 60 =

18) 50% of 90 =

19) 30% of 45 =

20) 60% of 150 =

✏ *Solve.*

21) A test has 20 questions. If peter gets 80% correct, how many questions did peter missed?

22) In a school, 25 % of the teachers teach basic math. If there are 50 basic math teachers, how many teachers are there in the school?

23) 24 students in a class took an algebra test. If 18 students passed the test, what percent do not pass?

24) Yesterday, there were 20 problems assigned for math homework. Lucy got 18 out of 20 problems correct. What percentage did Lucy get correct?

25) Megan's Tea Shop has caffeinated tea and decaffeinated tea. The tea shop served 10 teas in all, 7 of which were caffeinated. What percentage of the teas were caffeinated?

Converting Between Percent, Fractions, and Decimals

✍ *Converting fractions to decimals.*

1) $\frac{35}{100}$ 4) $\frac{46}{100}$ 7) $\frac{91}{100}$

2) $\frac{32}{100}$ 5) $\frac{72}{100}$ 8) $\frac{36}{100}$

3) $\frac{56}{100}$ 6) $\frac{21}{100}$ 9) $\frac{98}{100}$

✍ *Write each decimal as a percent.*

10) 0.72   13) 0.42   16) 1.3

11) 0.962   14) 0.83   17) 0.035

12) 0.54   15) 0.452   18) 3.12

✍ *How many percentages have the sizes changed?*

19)

20)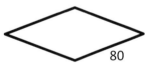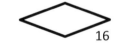

21)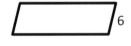

22)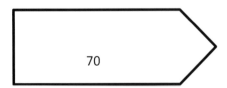

Percent Problems

✎ Solve each problem.

1) 60 is 120% of what?

2) 40% of what number is 50?

3) 27% of 142 is what number?

4) What percent of 125 is 30?

5) 30 is what percent of 120?

6) 44 is 25% of what?

7) 33 is 30% of what?

8) 52% of 150 is what?

9) 15 is what percent of 300?

10) What is 35% of 52 m?

11) What is 45% of 120 inches?

12) 18 inches is 40% of what?

✎ Solve.

13) Liam scored 21 out of 33 marks in Algebra, 37 out of 46 marks in science and 75 out of 95 marks in mathematics. In which subject his percentage of marks in best?

14) Ella require 50% to pass. If she gets 160 marks and falls short by 40 marks, what were the maximum marks she could have got?

15) There are 60 employees in a company. On a certain day, 36 were present. What percent showed up for work?

16) A metal bar weighs 24 ounces. 15% of the bar is gold. How many ounces of gold are in the bar?

17) A crew is made up of 12 women; the rest are men. If 20% of the crew are women, how many people are in the crew?

Find What Percentage a Number Is of Another

✍ *Find the percentage of the numbers.*

1) 10 is what percent of 40?

2) 12 is what percent of 240?

3) 151.2 is what percent of 270?

4) 14 is what percent of 112?

5) 6 is what percent of 30?

6) 17 is what percent of 85?

7) 39.6 is what percent of 88?

8) 420 is what percent of 350?

9) 13 is what percent of 104?

10) 9 is what percent of 225?

11) 75 is what percent of 50?

12) 11 is what percent of 55?

13) 300 is what percent of 1250?

14) 7.5 is what percent of 60?

15) 352is what percent of 220?

16) 504 is what percent of 252?

17) 52 is what percent of 260?

18) 45 is what percent of 360?

✍ *Solve*

19) Challenger Elementary School has 800 students. Every Wednesday, 12% of the students stay after school for Chess Club. How many students attend Chess Club on Wednesdays?

20) Anastasia is grocery shopping with her father and wonders how much shopping is left to do. "We already have 60% of the items on our list," her father says. Anastasia sees 12 items in the cart. How many grocery items are on the list?

21) A gumball machine contains 23 green gumballs, 52 red gumballs, 34 blue gumballs, 61 yellow gumballs, and 30 pink gumballs. What percentage of the gumballs are red?

Find a Percentage of a Given Number

✎ Find a Percentage of a Given Number.

1) 25% of 50 =

2) 40% of 90 =

3) 11% of 69 =

4) 12% of 60 =

5) 45% of 66 =

6) 38% of 55 =

7) 65% of 30 =

8) 15% of 40 =

9) 5% of 80 =

10) 20% of 80 =

11) 80% 0f 80 =

12) 25% of 36 =

13) 70% of 40 =

14) 45% of 60 =

15) 45% of 90 =

16) 40% of 120 =

17) 30% of 9 =

18) 65% of 200 =

19) 66% of 10 =

20) 36% of 50 =

21) 96% of 80 =

✎ Solve.

22) Luke and Matthew ran a lemonade stand on Saturday. They agreed that Matthew would get 60% of the profit because the lemonade stand was his idea. They made a profit of $25. How much money did Matthew make?

23) Mrs. Conley asks her class what kind of party they want to have to celebrate their excellent behavior. Out of all the students in the class, 5 want an ice cream party, 7 want a movie party, 10 want a costume party, and the rest are undecided. If 20% want an ice cream party, how many students are in the class?

24) There are 25 students in Ms. Nguyen's second-grade class. In the class election, 4 students voted for Benjamin, 12 voted for Sahil, and 9 voted for Maria. What percentage of the class voted for Maria?

Percent of Increase and Decrease

✍ *Find each percent change to the nearest percent. Increase or decrease.*

1) From 25 grams to 110 grams.

2) From 200 m to 50 m

3) From $520 to $102

4) From 256 ft. to 70 ft.

5) From 526 ft. to 800 ft.

6) From 25 inches to 125 inches

7) From 33 ft. to 163 ft.

8) From 536 miles to 76 miles

✍ *Solve.*

9) The population of a place in a particular year increased by 10%. Next year it decreased by 15%. Find the net increase or decrease percent in the initial population.

10) While measuring a line segment of length 5cm, it was measured 5.2cm by mistake. Find the percentage error in measuring the line segment.

11) A number is increased by 40% and then decreased by 40%. Find the net increase or decrease per cent.

12) The price of wheat increased by 10%. By how much per cent should mother reduce her consumption in the house so that her expenditure on wheat does not increase?

13) The football team at Riverside College plays in an old stadium that seats 31,780 people. This stadium will be demolished and a new one built that can hold 35% more fans. What will be the seating capacity of the new, bigger stadium?

Markup, Discount, and Tax

✍ *Find the selling price of each item.*

1) Cost of a pen: $4.5, markup:.25%, discount: 20%, tax:5%

2) Cost of a puppy: $210, markup:20%, discount:15%

3) Cost of a shirt: $18.00, markup:22%, discount:20%

4) Cost of an oil change: $28.5, markup:55%

5) Cost of computer: $1,690.00, markup:15%

✍ *Solve.*

6) Vanessa earns a base salary of $400.00 with an additional %5, percent commission on everything she sells. Vanessa sold $1650.00-dollar worth of items last week. What was Vanessa's total pay last week?

7) The pie store is having a %20 percent off sale on all its pies. If the pie you want regularly costs $18, how much would you save with the discount?

8) Zoe paid $18.60 in sales tax for purchasing a table. The sales tax rate is 12%, What was the price of Zoe's table before sales tax?

9) Daniel works at a nearby electronics store. He makes a commission of 15% on everything he sells. If he sells a laptop for $293.00, how much money does Daniel make in commission?

Answers of Worksheets

Percentage Calculations

1) 5	6) 25	11) 52	16) 120	21) 4
2) 12	7) 21	12) 15	17) 18	22) 200
3) 13	8) 19	13) 0	18) 45	23) 25%
4) 6	9) 10	14) 168	19) 13.5	24) 90%
5) 45	10) 75	15) 12	20) 90	25) 70%

Converting Between Percent, Fractions, and Decimals

1) 0.35	6) 0.21	11) 96.2%	16) 130%	21) 25%
2) 0.32	7) 0.91	12) 54%	17) 3.5%	22) 20%
3) 0.56	8) 0.36	13) 42%	18) 312%	
4) 0.46	9) 0.98	14) 83%	19) 75%	
5) 0.72	10) 72%	15) 45.2 %	20) 20%	

Percent Problems

1) 50	6) 176	11) 54 inches	15) 60%
2) 125	7) 110	12) 45inches	16) 3.6 ounces
3) 38.34	8) 78	13) science, 80%	17) 60
4) 24%	9) 5%	14) 400	
5) 25%	10) 18.2 m		

Find What Percentage a Number Is of Another

1) 25%	6) 20%	11) 150%	16) 200%	21) 26%
2) 5%	7) 45%	12) 20%	17) 20%	
3) 56%	8) 120%	13) 24%	18) 12.5%	
4) 12.5%	9) 12.5%	14) 12.5%	19) 96	
5) 20%	10) 4%	15) 160%	20) 20	

Find a Percentage of a Given Number

1) 12.5	6) 20.9	11) 64	16) 48	21) 76.8
2) 36	7) 19.5	12) 9	17) 2.7	22) 15
3) 7.59	8) 6	13) 28	18) 130	23) 25
4) 7.2	9) 4	14) 27	19) 6.6	24) 36
5) 29.7	10) 16	15) 40.5	20) 18	

Percent of Increase and Decrease

1) 440% increase	6) 500% increase	11) 16% decrease
2) 75% decrease	7) 493% increase	12) $9\frac{1}{10}\%$
3) 80.4% decrease	8) 86% decrease	13) 42,903
4) 73% decrease	9) 6.5% decrease	
5) 52% increase	10) 4%	

Markup, Discount, and Tax

1) $4.725	4) $44.175	7) 3.6
2) $214.2	5) $1943.5	8) 16.61
3) $17.568	6) $482.50	9) 43.95

Section 2: Algebra

- *Algebraic Expressions*

- *Equations and Inequalities*

- *Systems of Equations*

- *Linear Functions*

- *Monomials and Polynomials*

- *Exponents and Radicals*

Chapter 5:

Algebraic Expressions

Topics that you'll learn in this part:

- ✓ Expressions and Variables
- ✓ Simplifying Variable Expressions
- ✓ Simplifying Polynomial Expressions
- ✓ The Distributive Property
- ✓ Evaluating One Variable
- ✓ Evaluating Two Variables
- ✓ Combining like Terms

Expressions and Variables

✎*Simplify each expression.*

1) $3x + 2x$,

   Use $x = 4$

2) $3(-3x + 9) + 3x$,

   Use $x = 2$

3) $(2x + 5) + (-2x)$,

   Use $x = 4$

4) $(6x - 3)(2x + 1)$,

   Use $x = 2$

5) $(2x + 5) + (3y - 3)$,

   Use $x = 2, y = -2$

6) $(5x - 1)(2x + y)$,

   Use $x = -1, y = 3$

7) $(2y)(2y - 3x)$,

   Use $x = 2, y = 1$

8) $(5x + 2y)y$,

   Use $x = 4, y = 2$

9) $3x + 2(2y - 2)$,

   Use $x = 4, y = 2$

10) $x + x(y - x)$,

    Use $x = 1, y = 2$

11) $2 + y(y - 2x)$,

    Use $x = 3, y = 1$

12) $x(2y - 3x)$,

    Use $x = -2, y = 2$

✎*Simplify each expression.*

13) $2 + 2x - 3x =$

14) $4z + 2(z + 6) =$

15) $4y + 5 + 3y =$

16) $4w - 5 - 3w =$

17) $3m - 4(2m + 1) =$

18) $2t - 4(2 - t) =$

19) $-2k + 5 + 9k =$

20) $3(2d + 2) + (-6d) =$

21) $(-5)(5q + 3) - 3q =$

22) $(-a) + (-3)(1 - a) =$

23) $(2x - 1) - (6 - x) =$

24) $(-5)(2m + 2) + 3m =$

25) $9x - 4 - 5x + 3 =$

26) $(-3z) + (-2)(1 - z) =$

27) $14n - 3m + 12m - 19n =$

28) $33x - 5(6x - 1) =$

Simplifying Variable Expressions

✎ *Simplify each expression.*

1) $-6 - 2x^2 + 4x^2 =$

2) $3 + 10x^2 + 2 + 5x^2 =$

3) $4x^2 + 4(2x + 1) =$

4) $4x^2 - x(4x + 1) =$

5) $4(x^2 - 1) + 4x(2x + 1) =$

6) $(x^3 + 4) + x(2x^2 + 1) =$

7) $4x^2 - 19 + 4(2x^2 + 1) =$

8) $x^4 + 4(2x + 1) - 2x^4 =$

9) $(3x^2 + 1)x + (x^3 - x) =$

10) $(2x - 1)(2x + 1) =$

11) $(5x - 2)(5x + 2) =$

12) $(x + 4)(x + 4) =$

13) $2x^2 + 5x - 10x^2 - 2x =$

14) $32x - 15(2x + 2) =$

15) $(2x + 1)x + (-3x^2) - x =$

16) $2(2 - x) + 2(2x - 4) =$

17) $3(x + 9) =$

18) $(-6)(8x - 4) =$

19) $7x + 3 - 3x =$

20) $-2 - x^2 - 6x^2 =$

21) $3 + 10x^2 + 2 =$

22) $8x^2 + 6x + 7x^2 =$

23) $x^2 - 2x + 4x^2 - 1 =$

24) $x^3(2x - x^2 - 1) - x^5 =$

25) $Z^2 - Z(2Z + 5) =$

26) $4x^2 + 2x(3 - 5x) =$

27) $10m\left(\frac{m-15}{5}\right) + 4m =$

28) $3x^2 - 2x(4x + 1) =$

✎ *Simplify.*

29) $x(3x + 3), x = 2$

30) $4 - 5x + 9x - 3, x = 1$

31) $(2x + 3)(2x + 1), x = 2$

32) $x(3x - 14), x = 4$

33) $2x + 9 - 3x + 2, x = -2$

34) $x(x + 4) + 2x, x = 2$

35) $(15x - 25)x, x = 3$

36) $x + x(6x - 1), x = -1$

37) $x + (7 - x), x = 3$

38) $(3x - 1)(x + 2), x = -2$

Simplifying Polynomial Expressions

✍ *Simplify each polynomial.*

1) $(2x^3 + 5x^2) - (12x + 2x^2) =$

2) $(2x^5 + 2x^3) - (7x^3 + 6x^2) =$

3) $(12x^4 + 4x^2) - (2x^2 - 6x^4) =$

4) $14x - 3x^2 - 2(6x^2 + 6x^3) =$

5) $(5x^3 - 3) + 5(2x^2 - 3x^3) =$

6) $(4x^3 - 2x) - 2(4x^3 - 2x^4) =$

7) $2(4x - 3x^3) - 3(3x^3 + 4x^2) =$

8) $(2x^2 - 2x) - (2x^3 + 5x^2) =$

9) $2x^3 - (4x^4 + 2x) + x^2 =$

10) $x^4 - 2(x^2 + x) + 3x =$

11) $(2x^2 - x^4) - (4x^4 - x^2) =$

12) $4x^2 - 5x^3 + 15x^4 - 12x^3 =$

13) $2x^2 - 5x^4 + 14x^4 - 11x^3 =$

14) $2x^2 + 5x^3 - 7x^2 + 12x =$

15) $2x^4 - 5x^5 + 8x^4 - 8x^2 =$

16) $5x^3 + 15x - x^2 - 2x^3 =$

17) $14x^3 + 5 - 3(3x^2 + 1) =$

18) $2(3x + 1) + 2x(x - 2) =$

19) $-10x^2 + 4x^5 + 12x(1 + x) =$

20) $-3x - x^3 + x(3x + 3) =$

✍ *Solve.*

21) If $G = t^2 - 5t + 6$ and $H = -8t^2 + 7t - 9$ then what is the sum of sum G and H?

22) Subtract $6x^2 - 7x - 11$ from $5x^2 - 4x + 3$.

23) A polynomial of the $4th$ degree with a leading coefficient of 7 and a constant term of 8. Which answer is correct?

A: $7x^5 + 6x - 8$

B: $7x^4 + 6x + 8$

C: $7x^2 - 6x + 8$

D: $7x^4 + 8x + 7$

The Distributive Property

✍ *Use the distributive property to simply each expression.*

1) $x(3 - 2x) =$

2) $(-2)(2x - 1) + x =$

3) $3x(2 - x) =$

4) $(x + 1)(x - 1) =$

5) $(-5)(x + 3 - 3x) =$

6) $14(2x + 5) =$

7) $(x + 2)2x =$

8) $12(3x - 1) =$

9) $3x(x - 4) =$

10) $7x(1 + x) + 14 =$

11) $(-2x)x - 4x(4 + 5x) + 2 =$

12) $2x(4 - x) + (3x^2 + 4) =$

13) $(x + 1)(x - 1) + (-2x)x =$

14) $2x(x^2 + x + 1) + x(x - 1) =$

15) $3x(x - 1) - 3x(1 - x) =$

16) $(-2)(x - 1) + 10(x + 2) =$

17) $(3x + 1)(x - 1) + 2x^2 =$

18) $5(x + 1) + (-2x)(x + 2) =$

19) $x^2(x - 1) + x(2x^2 + 3) =$

20) $2(2 + 3x) =$

21) $3(5 + 5x) =$

22) $4(3x - 8) =$

23) $(6x - 2)(-2) =$

24) $(-3)(x + 2) =$

25) $(2 + 2x)5 =$

26) $(-4)(4 - 2x) =$

27) $-(-2 - 5x) =$

28) $(-6x + 2)(-1) =$

29) $(-5)(x - 2) =$

30) $-(7 - 3x) =$

31) $8(8 + 2x) =$

32) $2(12 + 2x) =$

33) $(-6x + 8)4 =$

34) $(3 - 6x)(-7) =$

35) $(-12)(2x + 1) =$

36) $(8 - 2x)9 =$

37) $5(7 + 9x) =$

38) $11(5x + 2) =$

39) $(-4x + 6)6 =$

40) $(3 - 6x)(-8) =$

41) $(-12)(2x - 3) =$

42) $(10 - 2x)9 =$

Evaluating One Variable

✎*Simplify each algebraic expression.*

1) $4 - (2x + 1), x = 3$

2) $3x + 5, x = 2$

3) $-2x - 7, x = -2$

4) $3x - 5, x = -3$

5) $3x + 6, x = 3$

6) $12x - 10, x = 2$

7) $1 - 2x + 4, x = -3$

8) $5 - 3x, x = -3$

9) $\frac{15}{x+4} - 3, x = -7$

10) $\frac{x+2}{4} + 2x, x = 6$

11) $\frac{3x(x-2)}{(x+6)}, x = 3$

12) $\frac{4x+2}{x} + 4x, x = 2$

13) $\frac{8}{x+1} - 12x, x = 3$

14) $2x + \frac{x}{8}, x = 8$

15) $(2x + 1) + 3x, x = -2$

16) $2x + \frac{x+3}{2}, x = 3$

17) $(5x - 1) + (3x + 2), x = 3$

18) $(-x)(5x - 4) + 2x, x = 3$

19) $4x + 5 + 2x - 2, x = 2$

20) $(-2x)(x - 1), x = -2$

21) $-3x + 5(3 - x), x = 4$

22) $\frac{3x+5}{1-x} + 2x, x = 3$

23) $\frac{2(2x-1)}{(1-x)+2x+1}, x = -4$

24) $\frac{2x+5}{x} + 4x, x = 5$

25) $3x - \frac{1-x}{1+x}, x = -5$

26) $4x + 2 - 6x, x = 1$

27) $\frac{2x+5+14x}{x(1-x)}, x = 2$

28) $\frac{3x(1-2x)}{x+2}, x = 3$

29) $3x^2 + 2x - 1, x = -2$

30) $\frac{32x-20}{x+4}, x = -3$

31) $\frac{12x-10}{2x}, x = 1$

32) $(3x - 4) - 5x, x = -3$

33) $\frac{-2x+1-x}{x-3}, x = -3$

34) $4x(x + 1) + x, x = -4$

35) $2t(5 - t), t = -5$

36) $-2y(3y + 4), y = -2$

37) $4m + \frac{3m-1}{m+1}, m = 3$

38) $(3y + 1) + (2y - 3), y = 0$

39) $5G(3 + 2G) - G, G = -1$

Evaluating Two Variables

🖎 *Simplify each algebraic expression.*

1) $2(x + 1) + y - 3 + 2,$

   $x = 3, y = 1$

2) $\left(-\frac{y+3}{x}\right) + 3y$

   $x = 5, y = 7$

3) $(-2a)(-2a - 2b),$

   $a = -2, b = 3$

4) $2(x - 2y),$

   $x = -2, y = 3$

5) $3x + 2 - 2y,$

   $x = 5, y = -2$

6) $2 + 2(-2x - 3y),$

   $x = 4, y = 1$

7) $12(x + y + 1) + y,$

   $x = -1, y = 3$

8) $(2x + 1)y$

   $x = 3, y = 2$

9) $(x + 12) \div 2y$

   $x = 2, y = -1$

10) $(2x + y)2y + 2,$

    $x = 2, y = 5$

11) $2(x + y) + 5y,$

    $x = 2, y = 3$

12) $4y(2x + y),$

    $x = -2, y = 2$

13) $2x + 5 - 3y,$

    $x = 2, y = -3$

14) $\frac{3x+5}{2y-2} + 2xy,$

    $x = -2, y = -1$

15) $3x + 2xy - 3y + 2,$

    $x = 4, y = 2$

16) $3y - \frac{42x}{2y} + 2y,$

    $x = 1, y = -3$

17) $2(2y - x) - 3(xy - 1),$

    $x = 2, y = -3$

18) $\frac{y}{-x} + 2xy + 3y,$

    $x = -3, y = -6$

19) $2x - 3y + 2(x - y),$

    $x = 4, y = -4$

20) $\frac{2x-y}{2x+y} - 2xy,$

    $x = -3, y = 2$

21) $4xy - 3x + y,$

    $x = 2, y = -1$

Combining like Terms

✍ *Simplify each expression.*

1) $3x + 2 - 5x + 1 =$

2) $2x(1 + x) + 2 =$

3) $2(x - 1) + 3x - 1 =$

4) $2(2 - x) + 2x + 2 =$

5) $5x + 2 + 7x + 3x =$

6) $x + 2(3x - 2) =$

7) $(x + 1)(x - 1) - 2x =$

8) $9x - 2 - 5x + 7 =$

9) $2(2x + 1) - 5x =$

10) $2 + 2x - 5x - 3 =$

11) $12x - 2(1 - x) =$

12) $(3 - x)(x - 1) =$

13) $x + 1 + 3x + 4x =$

14) $3x + 9x - 2x + 7 =$

15) $-12x + 3 - x(-3) =$

16) $3x + 5x - 4x + 10 =$

17) $5(x - 2) + x(12 - 4) =$

18) $32x - 4 - 17x - 2x =$

19) $22x + 14x + 2 - 18x =$

20) $(x + 3) + 3x + 5x - 2 =$

21) $2 - 8x + 3 + 5x =$

22) $33x - 12x + 2x =$

23) $2(3x - 2) + (-4x + 4) =$

24) $2x - 4x + 7x + 2 =$

25) $72x - 33x + (-20x) =$

26) $3 - 5x - 12x + 25x =$

27) $12x - 5 + 4x - 3 =$

28) $12x + 4x - 21 =$

29) $5 + 2x - 8 =$

30) $(-2x + 6)2 =$

31) $7 + 3x + 6x - 4 =$

32) $9(x - 7x) - 5 =$

33) $7(3x + 6) + 2x =$

34) $3x - 12 - 5x =$

35) $2(4 + 3x) - 7x =$

36) $22x + 6 + 2x =$

37) $(-5x) + 12 + 7x =$

38) $(-3x) - 9 + 15x =$

39) $2(5x + 7) + 8x =$

40) $2(9 - 3x) - 17x =$

41) $-4x - (6 - 14x) =$

42) $(-4) - (3)(5x + 8) =$

Answers of Worksheets

Expressions and Variables

1)	20	8)	48	15)	$7y + 5$	22)	$2a - 3$
2)	15	9)	16	16)	$w - 5$	23)	$3x - 7$
3)	5	10)	2	17)	$-5m - 4$	24)	$-7m - 10$
4)	45	11)	-3	18)	$6t - 8$	25)	$4x - 1$
5)	0	12)	-20	19)	$7k + 5$	26)	$-z - 2$
6)	-6	13)	$-x + 2$	20)	6	27)	$-5n + 9m$
7)	-8	14)	$6z + 12$	21)	$-28q - 15$	28)	$3x + 5$

Simplifying Variable Expressions

1)	$2x^2 - 6$	14)	$-2x - 30$	27)	$2m^2 - 26m$
2)	$15x^2 + 5$	15)	$-x^2$	28)	$-5x^2 - 2x$
3)	$4x^2 + 8x + 4$	16)	$2x - 4$	29)	18
4)	$-x$	17)	$3x + 27$	30)	5
5)	$12x^2 + 4x - 4$	18)	$-48x + 24$	31)	35
6)	$3x^2 + x + 4$	19)	$4x + 3$	32)	-8
7)	$12x^2 + x - 19$	20)	$-7x^2 - 2$	33)	13
8)	$-x^4 + 8x + 4$	21)	$10x^2 + 5$	34)	16
9)	$4x^3$	22)	$15x^2 + 6x$	35)	60
10)	$4x^2 - 1$	23)	$5x^2 - 2x - 1$	36)	6
11)	$25x^2 - 4$	24)	$-2x^5 + 2x^4 - x^3$	37)	7
12)	$x^2 + 8x + 16$	25)	$-Z^2 - 5Z$	38)	0
13)	$-8x^2 + 3x$	26)	$-6x^2 + 6x$		

Simplifying Polynomial Expressions

1)	$2x^3 + 3x^2 - 12x$	6)	$4x^4 - 4x^3 - 2x$	11)	$-5x^4 + 3x^2$
2)	$2x^5 - 5x^3 - 6x^2$	7)	$-15x^3 - 12x^2 + 8x$	12)	$15x^4 - 17x^3 + 4x^2$
3)	$18x^4 + 2x^2$	8)	$-2x^3 - 3x^2 - 2x$	13)	$9x^4 - 11x^3 + 2x^2$
4)	$-12x^3 - 15x^2 + 14x$	9)	$-4x^4 + 2x^3 + x^2 - 2x$	14)	$5x^3 - 5x^2 + 12x$
5)	$-10x^3 + 10x^2 - 3$	10)	$x^4 - 2x^2 + x$	15)	$-5x^5 + 10x^4 - 8x^2$

16) $3x^3 - x^2 + 15x$

17) $14x^3 - 9x^2 + 2$

18) $2x^2 + 2x + 2$

19) $4x^5 + 2x^2 + 12x$

20) $-x^3 + 3x^2$

21) $-7t^2 + 2t - 3$

22) $x^2 - 3x - 14$

23) B

The Distributive Property

1) $-2x^2 - 3x$

2) $-3x + 2$

3) $-3x^2 + 6x$

4) $x^2 - 1$

5) $10x - 15$

6) $28x + 70$

7) $2x^2 + 4x$

8) $36x - 12$

9) $3x^2 - 12x$

10) $7x^2 + 7x + 14$

11) $-22x^2 - 16x + 2$

12) $x^2 + 8x + 4$

13) $2x^2 - x - 1$

14) $2x^3 + 3x^2 + x$

15) $6x^2 - 6x$

16) $8x + 22$

17) $5x^2 - 2x - 1$

18) $-2x^2 + x + 5$

19) $3x^3 - x^2 + 3x$

20) $6x + 4$

21) $15x + 15$

22) $12x - 32$

23) $-12x + 4$

24) $-3x - 6$

25) $10x + 10$

26) $8x - 16$

27) $5x + 2$

28) $6x - 2$

29) $-5x + 10$

30) $3x - 7$

31) $16x + 64$

32) $4x + 24$

33) $-24x + 32$

34) $42x - 21$

35) $-24x - 12$

36) $-18x + 72$

37) $45x + 35$

38) $55x + 22$

39) $-24x + 36$

40) $48x - 24$

41) $-24x + 36$

42) $-18x + 90$

Evaluating one Variables

1) -3

2) 11

3) -3

4) -14

5) 15

6) 14

7) 11

8) 14

9) -8

10) 14

11) 1

12) 13

13) -34

14) 17

15) -9

16) 9

17) 25

18) -27

19) 15

20) -12

21) -17

22) -1

23) 9

24) 23

25) $-13\frac{2}{4}$

26) 0

27) $-\frac{37}{2}$

28) -9

29) 7

30) -116

31) 1

32) 2

33) $-\frac{5}{3}$

34) 44

35) -100

36) -8

37) 14

38) -2

39) -4

Evaluating Two Variables

1) 8	6) − 20	11) 25	16) − 8	21) −15
2) 19	7) 39	12) − 16	17) 5	
3) −8	8) 14	13) 18	18) 16	
4) − 16	9) − 7	14) $4\frac{1}{4}$	19) 36	
5) 21	10) 92	15) 24	20) 14	

Combining like Terms

1) $3 - 2x$

2) $2x^2 + 2x + 2$

3) $5x - 3$

4) 6

5) $15x + 2$

6) $7x - 4$

7) $x^2 - 4x + 1$

8) $4x + 5$

9) $2 - x$

10) $-3x - 1$

11) $14x - 2$

12) $-x^2 + 4x - 3$

13) $8x + 1$

14) $10x + 7$

15) $3 - 9x$

16) $4x + 10$

17) $13x - 10$

18) $13x - 4$

19) $18x + 2$

20) $9x + 1$

21) $5 - 3x$

22) $23x$

23) $2x$

24) $5x + 2$

25) $19x$

26) $8x + 3$

27) $16x - 8$

28) $16x - 21$

29) $2x - 3$

30) $-4x + 129x + 3$

31) $-54x - 5$

32) $23x + 42$

33) $-2x - 12$

34) $-x + 8$

35) $24x + 6$

36) $2x + 12$

37) $12x - 9$

38) $18x + 14$

39) $-23x + 18$

40) $10x - 6$

41) $-15x - 28$

Chapter 6:

Equations and Inequalities

Topics that you'll learn in this part:

✓ One–Step Equations

✓ One–Step Equation Word Problems

✓ Two–Step Equations

✓ Two–Step Equation Word Problems

✓ Multi–Step Equations

✓ Graphing Single–Variable Inequalities

✓ One–Step Inequalities

✓ Multi-Step Inequalities

One–Step Equations

⟋☙ *Solve each equation.*

1) $2x + 4 = 18$

2) $22 = (-8) + 3x$

3) $3x = (-30) + x$

4) $(-35) - x = (-6x)$

5) $(-6) = 4 + 10x$

6) $6 + 2x = (-2)$

7) $20x - 20 = (-220)$

8) $18 = 3x + 3$

9) $(-25) + 2 x = (-17)$

10) $5x + 5 = (-45)$

11) $3x - 12 = (-21)$

12) $x - 2 = (-8)$

13) $(-30) = x - 18$

14) $8 = 2x - 2$

15) $(-6x) - 6 = 36$

16) $(-55) = (-5x) + 10$

17) $2x - 15 = 25$

18) $8x - 16 = 32$

19) $24 = (-6x)$

20) $8x + 4 = 68$

21) $50x + 50 = 300$

⟋☙ *Write each sentence as an equation.*

22) Eight less than $\frac{1}{3}$ a number M is -13.

23) A number of multiplied by -12.3 is -73.

24) Twice a number, decreased by twenty-nine, is seven.

25) Thirty-two is twice a number increased by eight.

26) Twelve is sixteen less than four times a number.

27) The sum of eight and a number is five less than seventy.

28) Ten less than a number z is twenty-five.

29) Seven less than a number is sixty.

30) The sum of ten and a number is two less than thirty.

31) Seventeen less than a number x is fifty-three.

32) The sum of L and 15 is eight less than eighty-two.

33) The sum of eight and a number is ten less than eighteen.

One–Step Equation Word Problems

✎Solve.

1) Thira has read 110 pages of a 290-page book. She reads 20 pages each day. How many days will it take to finish?

2) You and a friend split the cost of a moped rental. Your friend pays the bill. You owe your friend only $12, because your friend owed you $9 from yesterday. How much was the total bill?

3) Mr. Herman's class is selling candy for a school fundraiser. The class has a goal of raising $500 by selling c boxes of candy. For every box they sell, they make$5.5. How many boxes of candy they need to sell?

4) Lindsey is helping her uncle plant an apple orchard. After picking up a truckload of trees, they plant 20 of them. The next day, they still have 50 trees left to plant. Find the total number of trees in the original truckload?

5) Tina is baking chocolate chip cookies for a party at school. She leaves 12 at home for her family and brings the remaining 24 cookies to school to share with her classmates. Find the total number of cookies that Tina bakes?

6) The Laughing Lollipop candy store is holding a raffle, and Preston wins the grand prize! He wins a gift card to the store, as well as a bag of giant lollipops. He gives 21 lollipops to his friends, and he keeps the remaining 3 lollipops. Find the total number of lollipops in the bag?

Two–Step Equations

📝**Solve each equation.**

1) $2(4 + x) = 20$

2) $(-2)(x + 3) = 42$

3) $3(2x - 4) = (-36)$

4) $6(2 - 2x) = 12$

5) $10(4x + 4) = (-60)$

6) $5(2x + 5) = 45$

7) $2(7 - 2x) = (-34)$

8) $(-4)(2x - 4) = 48$

9) $4(x - 5) = 8$

10) $\frac{2x - 10}{2} = 12$

11) $\frac{3x + 3}{9} = 10$

12) $15 = (-5)(3x - 6)$

13) $\frac{12 - x}{5} = 6$

14) $12 = (-12) + \frac{4x}{8}$

15) $\frac{24 + 3x}{4} = 9$

16) $(-2)(5 - 4x) = 70$

17) $(-11x) + 15 = 26$

18) $\frac{-24 - 8x}{6} = 8$

19) $\frac{2x - 12}{7} = 6$

20) $\frac{(-8) + 3x}{10} = \frac{2}{5}$

21) $\frac{2x + 2}{2} = 5$

📝**Fill in the blank with the appropriate number**

22) $6 = \frac{x}{\Box} + 2, x = 16$

23) $\Box + \frac{x}{4} = -5, x = 4$

24) $0 = 4 + \frac{n}{\Box}, n = -20$

25) $-1 = \frac{\Box + x}{6}, x = -11$

26) $\frac{m + \Box}{3} = 8, m = 15$

27) $2(n + 5) = \Box, n = -6$

28) $144 = \Box(x + 5), x = -17$

29) $10 - 6x = \Box, x = 19$

30) $\frac{x + 5}{\Box} = -1, x = 11$

31) $-10 = \Box + 5x, x = 0$

32) $-10 = 10(x - \Box), x = 8$

33) $\frac{x}{9} + \Box = -2, x = -9$

34) $7(9 + x) = \Box, x = 3$

35) $8 + \frac{x}{\Box} = 5, x = 12$

36) $-243 = \Box(10 + x), x = 17$

37) $-15 = (\Box)x + 10, x = 5$

38) $-4 = \frac{x}{\Box} - 5, x = 20$

Two–Step Equation Word Problems

✎ *Solve.*

1) Aliyah had $24 to spend on seven pencils. After buying them she had $10. How much did each pencil cost?

2) Maria bought seven boxes. A week later half of all her boxes were destroyed in a fire. There are now only 22 boxes left. With how many did she start?

3) Sara Wong spent half of his weekly allowance playing arcade games. To earn more money his parents let him weed the garden for $6.55. What is his weekly allowance if he ended with $11.01?

4) Rob had some paper with which to make note cards. On his way to his room he found two more pieces to use. In his room he cut each piece of paper in half. When he was done, he had 22 half-pieces of paper. With how many sheets of paper did he start?

5) The Cooking Club made some pies to sell during lunch to raise money for an end-of-year banquet. The cafeteria contributed two pies to the club. Each pie was then cut into seven pieces and sold. There was a total of 84 pieces to sell. How many pies did the club make?

6) Adam won 59 lollipops playing hoops at the county fair. At school he gave two to every student in his math class. He only has 3 remaining. How many students are in his class?

Multi–Step Equations

✎Solve each equation.

1) $2(2x - 1) = 10 + x$

2) $(-3)(2 - x) = 30 - 3x$

3) $2x + 14 = 3(10 + 2x)$

4) $3x - 24 = 2(10 - x) + x$

5) $10x + 4 = (-36) - x + x$

6) $12x + 1 = 8x - 59$

7) $15x - 12 - 12x = 7x$

8) $(-3x) + 2(x + 1) = 4(6 + x) + 3$

✎Solve.

9) Tickets to a fundraiser are $14 if purchased ahead of time and $25 if purchased at the door. The total amount raised from all ticket sales was $625. If eleven tickets were purchased at the door, how many tickets were purchased ahead of time?

10) On Friday, you raked leaves for 4 neighbors, on Saturday you raked leaves for 5 neighbors, and on Sunday you raked leaves for 3 neighbors. Over the three days you earned a total of $135. If you were paid the same amount at each house, write and solve an equation to determine how much you earned per house.

11) Your school is having a fundraiser. You are selling candy bars that have been donated by the Hershey Company. You set a personal goal of raising $200 for your school and met that goal. You sold a total of 120 candy bars and one neighbor gave you a $20 donation without taking any candy bars. Write and solve an equation to determine how much each candy bar sold for?

Graphing Single–Variable Inequalities

 Draw a graph for each inequality.

1) $x > 2$

2) $x < 5$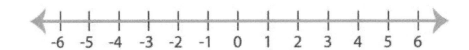

3) $x > -1$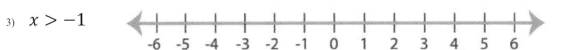

4) $x > 3$

5) $x < -5$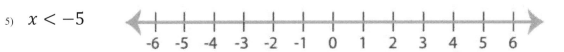

6) $x > -2$

7) $x < 0$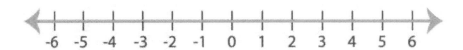

8) $x > 4$

One–Step Inequalities

✍ *Solve each inequality and graph it.*

1) $x + 2 \geq 3$
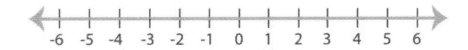

2) $x - 1 \leq 2$
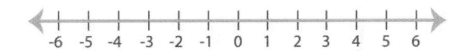

3) $2x \geq 12$
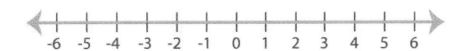

4) $4 + x \leq 5$

5) $x + 3 \leq -3$

6) $4x \geq 16$
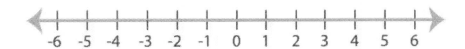

7) $9x \leq 18$
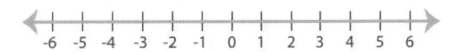

8) $x + 2 \geq 7$
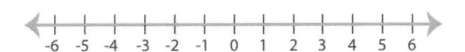

Multi-Step Inequalities

✍ *Solve each inequality.*

1) $x - 2 \leq 6$

2) $3 - x \leq 3$

3) $2x - 4 \leq 8$

4) $3x - 5 \geq 16$

5) $x - 5 \geq 10$

6) $2x - 8 \leq 6$

7) $8x - 2 \leq 14$

8) $-5 + 3x \leq 10$

9) $2(x - 3) \leq 6$

10) $7x - 5 \leq 9$

11) $4x - 21 < 19$

12) $2x - 3 < 21$

13) $17 - 3x \geq -13$

14) $9 + 4x < 21$

15) $3 + 2x \geq 19$

16) $6 + 2x < 32$

17) $4x - 1 < 7$

18) $3(3 - 2x) \geq -15$

19) $-(3 + 4x) < 13$

20) $20 - 8x \geq -28$

21) $-3(x - 7) > 21$

22) $\dfrac{2x + 6}{4} \leq 10$

23) $\dfrac{4x + 8}{2} \leq 12$

24) $\dfrac{3x - 8}{7} > 1$

25) $4 + \dfrac{x}{3} < 7$

26) $\dfrac{9x}{7} - 7 < 2$

27) $\dfrac{4x + 12}{4} > 1$

28) $15 + \dfrac{x}{5} < 12$

Answers of Worksheets

One–Step Equations

1) 7

2) 10

3) −15

4) 7

5) −1

6) −4

7) −10

8) 5

9) 4

10) −10

11) −3

12) −6

13) −12

14) 5

15) −5

16) 13

17) 20

18) 6

19) −4

20) 8

21) 5

22) $8 - \frac{1}{3}M = -13$

23) $(-12.3)f = -73$

24) $2x - 29 = 7$

25) $2x + 8 = 32$

26) $16 - 4x = 12$

27) $8 + x = 5 - 70$

28) $10 - z = 25$

29) $7 - x = 60$

30) $10 + x = 2 - 30$

31) $17 - x = 53$

32) $l + 15 = 8 - 82$

33) $8 + x = 10 - 8$

One–Step Equation Word Problems

1) 9

2) 42

3) 91

4) 30

5) 36

6) 24

Two–Step Equations

1) 6

2) −24

3) −4

4) 0

5) −2.5

6) 2

7) 12

8) −4

9) 7

10) 17

11) 29

12) 1

13) −18

14) 48

15) 4

16) 10

17) −1

18) −9

19) 27

20) 4

21) 4

22) 4

23) −6

24) 5

25) 5

26) 9

27) −2

28) −12

29) −104

30) −16

31) −10

32) −9

33) −1

34) 84

35) −4

36) −9

37) −1

38) 20

Two–Step Equation Word Problems

1) $2

2) 37

3) $8.92

4) 9

5) 10

6) 28

Multi–Step Equations

1) 4

2) 6

3) −4

4) 11

5) −4

6) −15

7) −3

8) −5

9) 25

10) 11.25

11) 1.5

Graphing Single–Variable Inequalities

1)

2)

3)

4)

5)

6)
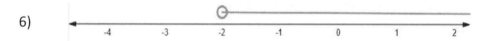

7)
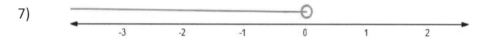

8)
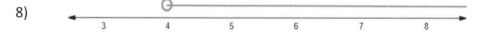

One–Step Inequalities

1)
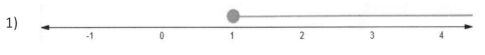

2)

3)

4)

5)

6)

7)

8)

Multi-Step Inequalities

1) $x \leq 8$

2) $x \geq 0$

3) $x \leq 6$

4) $x \geq 7$

5) $x \geq 15$

6) $x \leq 7$

7) $x \leq 2$

8) $x \leq 5$

9) $x \leq 6$

10) $x \leq 2$

11) $x < 10$

12) $x < 12$

13) $x \leq 10$

14) $x < 3$

15) $x \geq 8$

16) $x < 13$

17) $x < 2$

18) $x \leq 4$

19) $x > -4$

20) $x \leq 6$

21) $x < 0$

22) $x \leq 17$

23) $x \leq 4$

24) $x > 5$

25) $x < 9$

26) $x < 7$

27) $x > -2$

28) $x < -15$

Chapter 7:

Systems of Equations

Topics that you'll learn in this part:

✓ Solving Systems of Equations by Substitution

✓ Solving Systems of Equations by Elimination

✓ Systems of Equations Word Problems

Solving Systems of Equations by Substitution

✎ **Solve each system of equation by substitution.**

1) $\begin{cases} x + 4 = y \\ 2x + y = 1 \end{cases}$

2) $\begin{cases} 2x + y = 2 \\ x - y = 10 \end{cases}$

3) $\begin{cases} 4y - 2 = x \\ x + 2y = 4 \end{cases}$

4) $\begin{cases} 1 - x = 2y \\ 2x - 2y = -16 \end{cases}$

5) $\begin{cases} 3x - y = 6 \\ 2x + y = 14 \end{cases}$

6) $\begin{cases} 2x + 1 = 1 - y \\ x - 3y = 28 \end{cases}$

7) $\begin{cases} y - 3x = 4 \\ 2(x + y) + 5 = -11 \end{cases}$

8) $\begin{cases} 9 - 6x = 3y \\ 3x + y = 1 \end{cases}$

9) $\begin{cases} y = 7x - 10 \\ y = -3 \end{cases}$

10) $\begin{cases} y = -8x \\ 2x + 4y = 0 \end{cases}$

11) $\begin{cases} 6x - 11 = y \\ -2x - 3y = -7 \end{cases}$

12) $\begin{cases} 2x - 3y = -1 \\ x - 1 = y \end{cases}$

13) $\begin{cases} -3x - 3y = 3 \\ -5x - 17 = y \end{cases}$

14) $\begin{cases} y = -3x + 5 \\ 5x - 4y = -3 \end{cases}$

15) $\begin{cases} y - 5x = -7 \\ 12 - 2y = 3x \end{cases}$

16) $\begin{cases} y = 6 + 4x \\ -5x - y = 21 \end{cases}$

17) $\begin{cases} -7x - 2y = -13 \\ x - 2y = 11 \end{cases}$

18) $\begin{cases} -5x + y = -2 \\ 12 + 6y = 3x \end{cases}$

19) $\begin{cases} 3 + y - 5x = 0 \\ 3x - 8y = 24 \end{cases}$

20) $\begin{cases} x + 3y = 1 \\ -3x - 3y = -15 \end{cases}$

21) $\begin{cases} -3x - 8y = 20 \\ -5x + y = 19 \end{cases}$

22) $\begin{cases} 3y - 3x = 3 \\ y - 5x = 13 \end{cases}$

23) $\begin{cases} 6x + 6y = -6 \\ 5x + y = -13 \end{cases}$

24) $\begin{cases} 2x + y = 20 \\ 6x - 5y = 12 \end{cases}$

25) $\begin{cases} -3x - 4y = 2 \\ 3x + 3y = -3 \end{cases}$

26) $\begin{cases} -2x + 6y = 6 \\ -7x + 8y = -5 \end{cases}$

27) $\begin{cases} 4x + y = 24 \\ y = 4x + 24 \end{cases}$

28) $\begin{cases} -5x + 2y = 9 \\ y = 7x \end{cases}$

29) $\begin{cases} -7x - 6y - 4 = 0 \\ x - 8 = -3y \end{cases}$

30) $\begin{cases} -4x = 20 - 7y \\ y = 3x + 15 \end{cases}$

Solving Systems of Equations by Elimination

✍ *Solve each system of equation by elimination.*

1) $\begin{cases} -4x - 2y = -12 \\ 4x + 8y = -24 \end{cases}$

2) $\begin{cases} 4x + 8y = 20 \\ -4x + 2y = -30 \end{cases}$

3) $\begin{cases} x - y = 11 \\ 2x + y = 19 \end{cases}$

4) $\begin{cases} -6x + 5y = 1 \\ 6x + 4y = -10 \end{cases}$

5) $\begin{cases} -2x + 9y = -25 \\ -4x - 9y = -23 \end{cases}$

6) $\begin{cases} 8x + y = -16 \\ -3x + y = -5 \end{cases}$

7) $\begin{cases} -6x + 6y = 6 \\ -6x + 3y = -12 \end{cases}$

8) $\begin{cases} 7x + 2y = 24 \\ 8x + 2y = 30 \end{cases}$

9) $\begin{cases} 5x + y = 9 \\ 10x - 7y = -18 \end{cases}$

10) $\begin{cases} -4x + 9y = 9 \\ x - 3y = -6 \end{cases}$

11) $\begin{cases} -3x + 7y = -16 \\ -9x + 5y = 16 \end{cases}$

12) $\begin{cases} -7x + y = -19 \\ -2x + 3y = -19 \end{cases}$

13) $\begin{cases} 16x - 10y = 10 \\ -8x - 6y = 6 \end{cases}$

14) $\begin{cases} 8x + 14y = 4 \\ -6x - 7y = -10 \end{cases}$

15) $\begin{cases} -4x - 15y = -17 \\ -x + 5y = -13 \end{cases}$

16) $\begin{cases} -x - 7y = 14 \\ -4x - 14y = 28 \end{cases}$

17) $\begin{cases} -7x - 8y = 9 \\ -4x + 9y = -22 \end{cases}$

18) $\begin{cases} 5x + 4y = -30 \\ 3x - 9y = -18 \end{cases}$

19) $\begin{cases} -4x - 2y = 14 \\ -10x + 7y = -25 \end{cases}$

20) $\begin{cases} 3x - 2y = 2 \\ 5x - 5y = 10 \end{cases}$

21) $\begin{cases} 5x + 4y = -14 \\ 3x + 6y = 6 \end{cases}$

22) $\begin{cases} 2x + 10y = 6 \\ -5x - 20y = -15 \end{cases}$

23) $\begin{cases} -7x - 20y = -14 \\ 10y + 4 = 2x \end{cases}$

24) $\begin{cases} 3 + 2x = y \\ -3 - 7y = 10x \end{cases}$

25) $\begin{cases} -10x + 3y = 5 \\ x - y = -4 \end{cases}$

26) $\begin{cases} 12x - 5y = -20 \\ y = x + 4 \end{cases}$

27) $\begin{cases} -4x + 11y = 15 \\ x - 2y = 0 \end{cases}$

28) $\begin{cases} 7x - 3y = 20 \\ y = 5x - 4 \end{cases}$

29) $\begin{cases} -5x + 4y = 3 \\ x + 15 = 2y \end{cases}$

30) $\begin{cases} 8x + 5y = 24 \\ y = -4x \end{cases}$

Systems of Equations Word Problems

✎*Solve.*

1) A used book store also started selling used CDs and videos. In the first week, the store sold a combination of 40 CDs and videos. They charged $4 per CD and $6 per video and the total sales were $180. Determine the total number of CDs and videos sold.

2) At the end of the 2000-2001 football season, 31 Super Bowl games had been played with the current two football leagues, the American Football Conference (AFC) and the National Football Conference (NFC). The NFC won five more games than the AFC. Determine the total number of wins by each conference.

3) The length of Sally's garden is 4 meters greater than 3 times the width. The perimeter of her garden is 72 meters. Find the dimensions of Sally's garden.

4) Giselle works as a carpenter and as a blacksmith. She earns $20 as a carpenter and $25 as a blacksmith. Last week, Giselle worked both jobs for a total of 30 hours and earned a total of $690. How long did Giselle work as a carpenter last week, and how long did she work as a blacksmith?

5) At a sale on winter clothing, Cody bought two pairs of gloves and four hats for $43.00. Tori bought two pairs of gloves and two hats for $30.00. Find the prices of the hats and gloves.

Answers of Worksheets

Solving Systems of Equations by Substitution

1) $(-1, 3)$
2) $(4, -6)$
3) $(2, 1)$
4) $(-5, 3)$
5) $(4, 6)$
6) $(4, -8)$
7) $(-3, -5)$
8) $(-2, 7)$

9) $(1, -3)$
10) $(0, 0)$
11) $(2, 1)$
12) $(4, 3)$
13) $(-4, 3)$
14) $(1, 2)$
15) $(2, 3)$
16) $(-3, -6)$

17) $(3, -4)$
18) $(0, -2)$
19) $(0, -3)$
20) $(7, -2)$
21) $(-4, -1)$
22) $(-3, -2)$
23) $(-3, 2)$
24) $(7, 6)$

25) $(-2, 1)$
26) $(3, 2)$
27) $(0, 24)$
28) $(1, 7)$
29) $(-4, 4)$
30) $(-5, 0)$

Solving Systems of Equations by Elimination

1) $(6, -6)$
2) $(7, -1)$
3) $(10, -1)$
4) $(-1, -1)$
5) $(8, -1)$
6) $(-1, -8)$
7) $(5, 6)$
8) $(6, -9)$

9) $(1, 4)$
10) $(9, 5)$
11) $(-4, -4)$
12) $(2, -5)$
13) $(0, -1)$
14) $(4, -2)$
15) $(8, -1)$
16) $(0, -2)$

17) $(1, -2)$
18) $(-6, 0)$
19) $(-1, -5)$
20) $(-2, -4)$
21) $(-6, 4)$
22) $(3, 0)$
23) $(2, 0)$
24) $(-1, 1)$

25) $(1, 5)$
26) $(0, 4)$
27) $(10, 5)$
28) $(-1, -9)$
29) $(9, 12)$
30) $(-2, 8)$

Systems of Equations Word Problems

1) $(10 \text{ } videos, 30 CDs)$
2) $(NFC \text{ } wins \text{ } 18, AFC \text{ } wins 13)$
3) $(8, 28)$

4) $(12, 18)$
5) $(gloves: \$6, hats: \$8.5)$

Chapter 8:

Linear Functions

Topics that you'll learn in this part:

✓ Finding Slope

✓ Graphing Lines Using Slope–Intercept Form

✓ Graphing Lines Using Standard Form

✓ Writing Linear Equations

✓ Graphing Linear Inequalities

✓ Finding Midpoint

✓ Finding Distance of Two Points

✓ Slope and Rate of Change

✓ Find the Slope, X–intercept and Y–intercept

✓ Write an Equation from a Graph

✓ Slope–intercept form

✓ Point–slope form

✓ Equations of horizontal and vertical lines

✓ Equation of parallel or perpendicular lines

Finding Slope

✎*Find the slope of the line through each pair of points.*

1) $(0,2),(-3,2)$

2) $(2,2),(-3,-2)$

3) $(0,0),(4,-2)$

4) $(2,5),(1,1)$

5) $(15,8),(15,-8)$

6) $(-2,0),(1,3)$

7) $(-2,-4),(2,3)$

8) $(-2,-4),(-1,0)$

9) $(-6,5),(-1,0)$

10) $(-6,10),(4,0)$

11) $(15,5),(-5,1)$

12) $(-10,-2),(0,3)$

13) $(5,-2),(3,3)$

14) $(5,0),(10,10)$

15) $(0,2),(2,10)$

16) $(0,0),(-10,10)$

17) $(-22,-12),(-5,5)$

18) $(0,0),(-10,30)$

19) $(12,12),(-3,6)$

20) $(-6,2),(-4,6)$

21) $(-2,7),(-8,7)$

22) $(14,70),(28,7)$

23) $(9,6),(-1,-1)$

24) $(0,6),(12,24)$

✎*Solve.*

25) Some building codes require the slope of a stairway to be no steeper than 0.88 or $\frac{22}{25}$. The stairs in the Adam's house measure 11-inch-deep and 6 inch high. Do the stairs meet the code requirement?

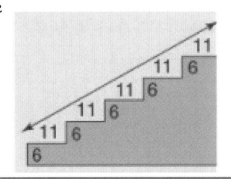

Graphing Lines Using Slope–Intercept Form

✎*Sketch the graph of each line.*

1) $y = \frac{1}{2}x - 4$

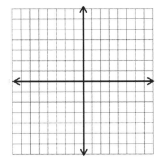

2) $y = x + 1$

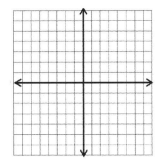

3) $y = -x + 1$

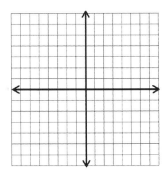

4) $y = 3x - 1$

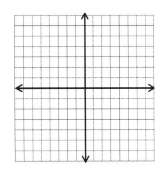

5) $y = -\frac{1}{5}x + \frac{1}{3}$

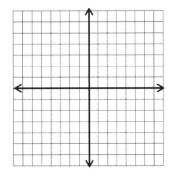

6) $y = \frac{3}{5}x - 1$

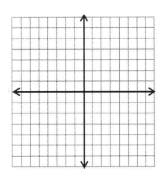

Graphing Lines Using Standard Form

✍Sketch the graph of each line.

1) $2x - 2y = 4$

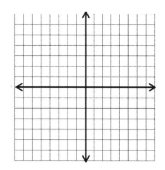

2) $3x + y = 2$

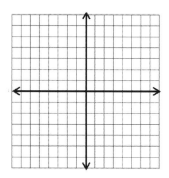

3) $x - y = 10$

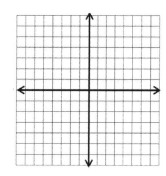

4) $3x + 2y = 2$

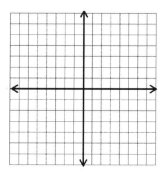

5) $y - 2x = 6$

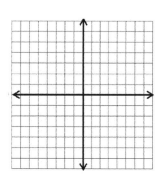

6) $2x - 3y = 6$

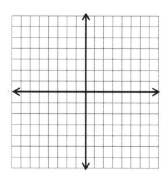

Writing Linear Equations

✍ *Write the slope–intercept form of the equation of the line through the given points.*

1) through: $(0, 2), (2, 4)$

2) through: $(0, 1), (2, -3)$

3) through: $(0, 2), (-2, -4)$

4) through: $(0, 2), (2, -8)$

5) through: $(0, 4), (-8, 0)$

6) through: $(1, 0), (0, -3)$

7) through: $(0, -2), (3, 0)$

8) through: $(0, 1), (-1, -3)$

9) through: $(1, -1), (1, 5)$

10) through: $(0, -0.5), (2, 3.5)$

11) through: $(0, 5), (-3, -4)$

12) through: $(5, 0), (0, 5)$

13) through: $(1, -6), (1.5, 0)$

14) through: $(0, 2), (1, -7)$

15) through: $(0, 3), (3, -3)$

16) through: $(0, 6), (5, -4)$

17) through: $(0, 3), (2, -5)$

18) through: $(4, 3), (2, 6)$

19) through: $(0, 1), (-4, 11)$

20) through: $(1.5, 2), (4, 5.5)$

✍ *Write the line slope from graph.*

21)

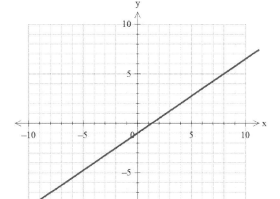

22)

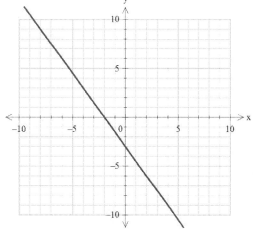

Graphing Linear Inequalities

✎Sketch the graph of each linear inequality.

1) $y > 3x + 4$

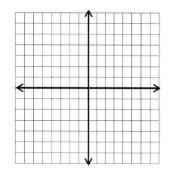

2) $y < -2x - 1$

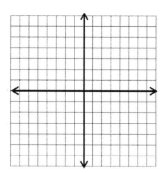

3) $y + \frac{1}{2} \geq \frac{1}{2}x$

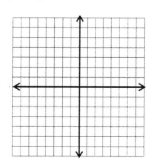

4) $y \leq 3 - 2x$

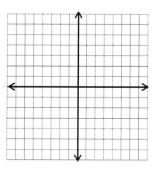

5) $4x - 2 \leq y$

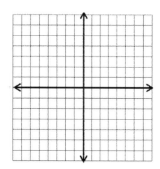

6) $1 - y \geq x$

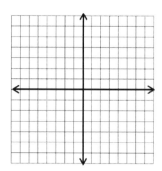

Finding Midpoint

✎ *Find the midpoint of the line segment with the given endpoints.*

1) $(-4, 5), (3, -\frac{1}{2})$

2) $(3, 7), (5, -3)$

3) $(-4, -2), (1, -10)$

4) $(3, -\frac{3}{2}), (4, 2)$

5) $(7, 0), (0, -10)$

6) $(4, -9), (0, 0)$

7) $(-3, -10), (3, 3)$

8) $(9, 1), (4, 4)$

9) $(75, 80), (40, 0)$

10) $(0, 13), (13, 0)$

11) $(-10, -3), (15, 14)$

12) $(33, 13), (9, 11)$

13) $(15, 0), (-10, -1)$

14) $(-3, 3), (15, 20)$

15) $(1, 10), (33, 0.5)$

16) $(90, -90), (50, 0)$

✎ *Solve.*

17) Find the midpoint of $\overline{AB}$ using the information in the diagram.

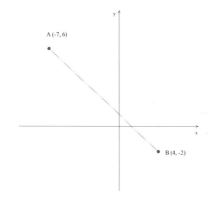

18) See the diagram. Find the midpoint of $\overline{BC}$.

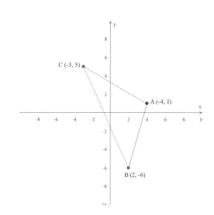

Finding Distance of Two Points

✏️ *Find the distance between each pair of points.*

1) $(5, 7), (5, 3)$

2) $(6, 0), (-4, -10)$

3) $(-2, 1), (10, -5)$

4) $(33, -5), (17, 8)$

5) $(-6, -5), (6, 5)$

6) $(0, 0), (5, 8)$

7) $(3, 4), (0, 0)$

8) $(12, 16) (0, 0)$

9) $(-17, 1), (2, -6)$

10) $(-3, 0), (14, 0)$

✏️ *Solve.*

11) Camp Sunshine is also on the lake. Use the Pythagorean Theorem to find the distance between Gabriela's house and Camp Sunshine to the nearest tenth of a meter.

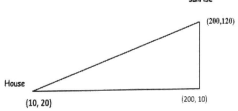

12) The class of math is mapped on a coordinate grid with the origin being at the center point of the hall. Mary's seat is located at the point (-4,7) and Betty's seat is located at (-2, 5). How far is it from Mary's seat to Betty's seat?

13) The teaching building of a university is mapped on a coordinate grid with the origin being at library. Math's building is located at the point (1,5) and History's building is located at (4, 9). How far is it from Math's building to History's building?

Slope and Rate of Change

🖎 **Find the slope of the line that passes through the points.**

1) $(-10, 4), (0, 2)$

2) $(3, 1), (12, 0)$

3) $(15, 0), (2, 13)$

4) $(12, 97), (-3, -5)$

5) $(-10, -8), (3, 1)$

6) $(-17, 20), (-1, -1)$

7) $(-2, -2), (0, 8)$

8) $(15, -8), (-1, 8)$

9) $(13, 0), (-3, 11)$

10) $(4, 3), (5, 1)$

11) $(12, 3), (-4, 3)$

12) $(1, -1), (0, 0)$

🖎 **Find the value of r so the line that passes through each pair of points has the given slope.**

13) $(1, 1), (2, r), m = 2$

14) $(-1, r), (0, 3), m = 1$

15) $(3, -1), (r, 3), m = -4$

16) $(r, -1), (0, 5), m = 3$

17) $(5, 1), (2, r), m = -1$

18) $(-3, 1), (r, 4), m = 3$

19) $(6, 2), (r, 4), m = 2$

20) $(6, r), (3, 4), m = -3$

21) $(12, -9), (r, -8), m = -1$

22) $(7, r), (5, -2), m = 3$

23) $(1, 1), (r, 5), m = 2$

24) $(7, r), (5, 10), m = -11$

25) $(1, 1), (r, 5), m = 2$

26) $(4, r), (-3, -8), m = \frac{2}{7}$

27) $(7, -12), (5, r), m = -11$

28) $(19, 3), (20, r), m = 0$

29) $(15, 8), (r, 9), m = -\frac{1}{32}$

30) $(r, -12), (15, -3), m = 1$

31) $(3, 1), (r, -5), m = -\frac{3}{2}$

32) $(3, -2), (-7, r), m = -1$

33) $(20, r), (-20, -10), m = 0.875$

34) $(6, 0), (r, -2), m = 0.2$

35) $(200, 100), (100, r), m = -1$

36) $(0, r), (10, 0), m = -0.5$

37) $(2, -8), (-10, r), m = -0.5$

Find the Slope, x–intercept and y–intercept

✎ *Find the* x *and* y *intercepts for the following equations.*

1) $x + 2y = -2$

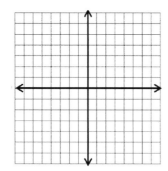

2) $y = 2x - 3$

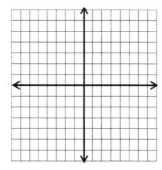

3) $-3x = 3y + 1$

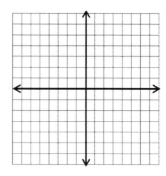

4) $2 - 2y = -5x$

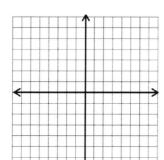

5) $-5x + 2y = 10$

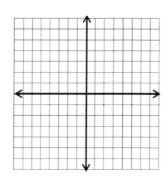

6) $2y = 2 - x$

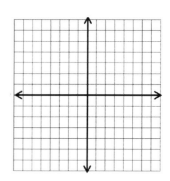

7) $1 - 2y = 7x$

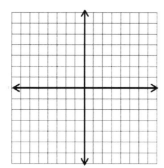

8) $2x + 4y = 9$

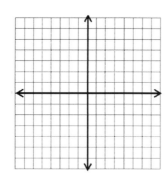

9) $3y = 7 + 2x$

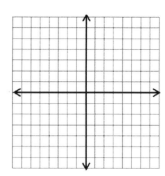

Write an equation from a graph

📝 *Write the slope intercept form of the equation of each line.*

1)

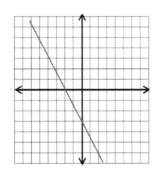

2)

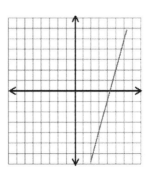

3)

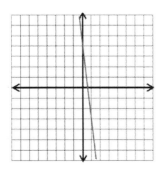

4)

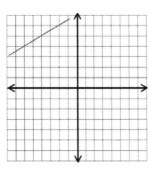

5)

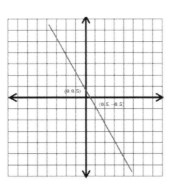

6)

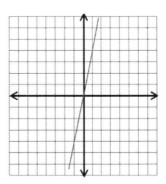

Slope–intercept Form

✎**Write the slope–intercept form of the equation of each line.**

1) $3x - 12 = 12y$

2) $2x - 3y = 6$

3) $\frac{-3}{2}x + 5y = 5$

4) $3(2x + y) = 6$

5) $14x + 7y = 28$

6) $3x - 4y = 5y + 1$

7) $3x + 4y = 3 + y$

8) $4 - 2x + y = 2$

9) $3x - y = 2$

10) $4y - 5x = -5$

11) $7x + 4y = 14 - 3y$

12) $15y - 5x = 30$

✎**Solve.**

13) Suppose that the water level of a river is 34 feet and that it is receding at a rate of 0.5 foot per day. Find the slope and write a sentence to interpret the slope in detail. Write an equation for the water level, L, after d days. In how many days will the water level be 26 feet?

14) For babysitting, Nicole charges a flat fee of $3, plus $5 per hour. Write an equation for the cost, C, after h hours of babysitting. What do you think the slope and the y-intercept represent? How much money will she make if she baby-sits 5 hours?

15) In order to "curve" a set of test scores, a teacher uses the equation $y = 2.5x + 10$, where y is the curved test score and x is the number of problems answered correctly. Find the test score of a student who answers 32 problems correctly. Explain what the slope and the y-intercept mean in the equation.

Point–slope Form

✎ *Find the slope of the following lines. Name a point on each line.*

1) $y = 3(x + 3)$

2) $y = 3x - 2$

3) $y = 4x + 3$

4) $y = \frac{2}{3}x - 1$

5) $y + 3 = 4x + 8$

6) $2y = 3x - 4$

7) $y - 1 = 4x - 2$

8) $3y - 4 = 2x$

9) $y + 1 = 3x - 3$

10) $4y - 8 = 4x + 10$

11) $y + 1 = 32(x + 1)$

12) $15x + 3 = 3y$

✎ *Write an equation in point–slope form for the line that passes through the given point with the slope provided.*

13) $(3,2), m = \frac{1}{2}$

14) $(1, -2), m = 3$

15) $(3, -2), m = -2$

16) $(4,1), m = 3$

17) $(-2, -3), m = -\frac{1}{2}$

18) $\left(\frac{3}{4}, -\frac{1}{2}\right), m = 3$

19) $(-2,0) m = \frac{3}{4}$

20) $\left(-\frac{3}{7}, \frac{1}{2}\right), m = 2$

21) $(0,2), m = 5$

22) $(-3,1), m = \frac{4}{5}$

23) $\left(-\frac{2}{3}, \frac{2}{3}\right), m = 4$

24) $(5,0), m = \frac{1}{5}$

25) $(3,3), m = 10$

26) $(-6, -5), m = -1$

27) $(-6,0), m = -\frac{2}{3}$

28) $(1,1), m = -4$

29) $(-3,2), m = -4$

30) $\left(-\frac{1}{2}, \frac{1}{4}\right), m = \frac{1}{2}$

31) $(-4,2), m = \frac{7}{3}$

32) $(0,1), m = \frac{1}{2}$

33) $(4,1), m = 2$

34) $(3,3), m = -1$

35) $(-1,0), m = -2$

36) $(6,5), m = 4$

37) $(1, -2), m = 3$

Equations of Horizontal and Vertical Lines

✎*Sketch the graph of each line.*

1) $y = 0$

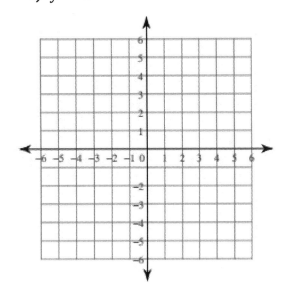

2) $y = 2$

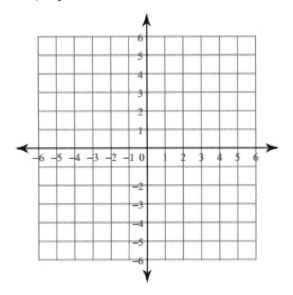

3) $x = -4$

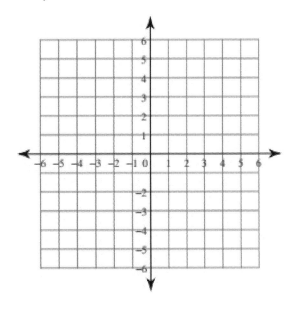

4) $x = 3$

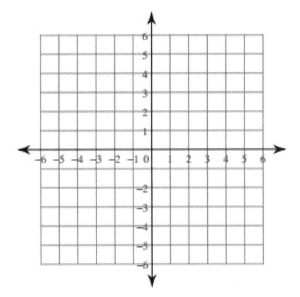

Equation of Parallel or Perpendicular Lines

✍ *Write an equation of the line that passes through the given point and is parallel to the given line.*

1) $(-2,3), 2y + 1 = 3x$

2) $(0,7), 3y + x = 2$

3) $(6,-1), 3y - x = 1$

4) $(-2,4), y + 2x = 2$

5) $(3,2), 2y + x = -2$

6) $(1,6) - 2y = x + 1$

7) $(3,2), y = 1 - x$

8) $(2,2), y = 3x$

9) $(-3,0), y = 2x - 2$

10) $(-3,2), 3y - 2 = 3x$

✍ *Write an equation of the line that passes through the given point and is perpendicular to the given line.*

11) $(-2,1), y + 1 = 3x$

12) $(0,-7), y + 2x = 2$

13) $(0,-1), 2y - 2x = 1$

14) $(-3,3), 2y + 2x = 2$

15) $(5,0), 3x + y = 5$

16) $(1,2), y = 3x + 1$

17) $(-3,0), 2y + 3 = x$

18) $(4,3), y = -5x + 1$

✍ *Solve.*

19) A caterer charges \$120 to cater a party for 15 people and \$200 for 25 people. Assume that the cost, y, is a linear function of the number of x people. Write an equation in slope-intercept form for this function. What does the slope represent? How much would a party for 40 people cost?

A. \$280

B. \$330

C. \$300

D. \$320

Answers of Worksheets

Finding Slope

1) 0	6) 1	11) 0.2	16) −1	21) 0
2) 0.8	7) 1.75	12) 0.5	17) 1	22) −4.5
3) −0.5	8) 4	13) −2.5	18) −3	23) 0.7
4) 4	9) −1	14) 2	19) 0.4	24) 1.5
5) Undefined	10) −1	15) 4	20) 2	25) 2.5

Graphing Lines Using Slope–Intercept Form

1)

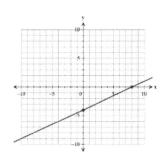

2)

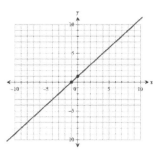

3)

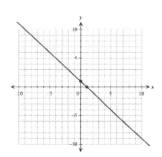

4)

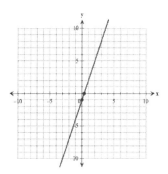

5)

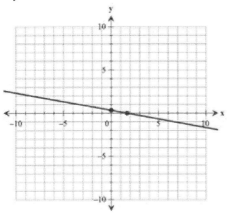

6)

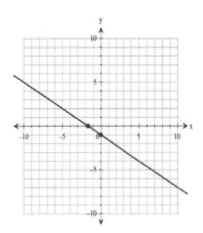

Graphing Lines Using Standard Form

1)

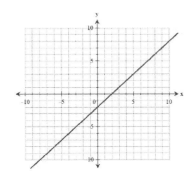

2)

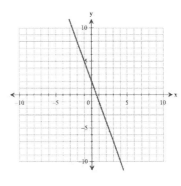

3)

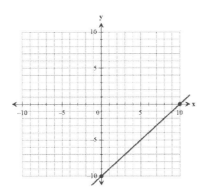

4)

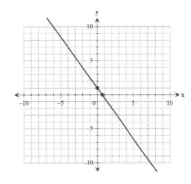

5)

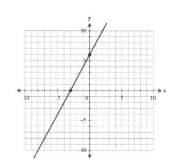

6)

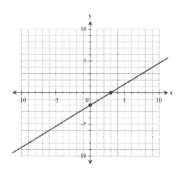

Writing Linear Equations

1) $y = x + 2$

2) $y = 1 - 2x$

3) $y = 3x + 2$

4) $y = 2 - 5x$

5) $y = \frac{1}{2}x + 4$

6) $y = 3x - 3$

7) $y = \frac{2}{3}x - 2$

8) $y = 4x + 1$

9) $x = 1$

10) $y = 2x - \frac{1}{2}$

11) $y = 3x + 5$

12) $y = -x + 5$

13) $y = 12x - 18$

14) $y = -9x + 2$

15) $y = 3 - 2x$

16) $y = 6 - 2x$

17) $y = 3 - 4x$

18) $y = 9 - \frac{3}{2}x$

19) $y = 1 - 2\frac{1}{2}x$

20) $y = 1.4x - 0.1$

21) $y = 0.75x - 1$

22) $y = -1.5x - 3$

Graphing Linear Inequalities

1)

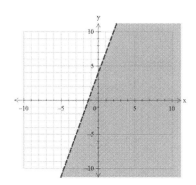

2)

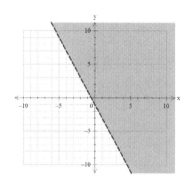

3)

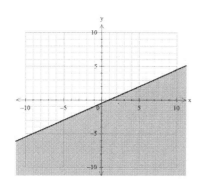

4)

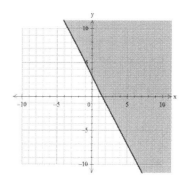

5)

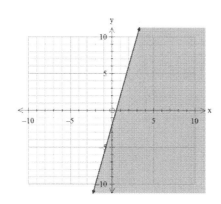

6)

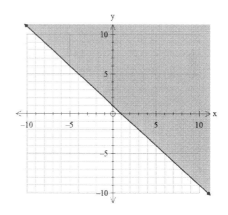

Finding Midpoint

1) $(-0.5, 2.25)$ 6) $(2, -4.5)$ 11) $(2.5, 5.5)$ 16) $(70, -45)$

2) $(4, 2)$ 7) $(0, -3.5)$ 12) $(21, 12)$ 17) $(-1.5, 2)$

3) $(-1.5, -6)$ 8) $(6.5, 2.5)$ 13) $(2.5, -0.5)$ 18) $(-0.5, -0.5)$

4) $(3.5, 0.25)$ 9) $(57.5, 40)$ 14) $(6, 11.5)$

5) $(3.5, -5)$ 10) $(6.5, 6.5)$ 15) $(17, 5.25)$

Finding Distance of Two Points

1) 4   4) 20.62   7) 5   10) 17   13) 5

2) 14.14   5) 15.62   8) 20   11) 214.7

3) 13.41   6) 9.43   9) 20.25   12) $2\sqrt{2}$

Slope and Rate of Change

1) -0.2	8) -1	16) -2	24) -12	32) 8
2) $-\frac{1}{9}$	9) $-\frac{11}{16}$	17) 4	25) 3	33) 25
3) -1	10) -2	18) -2	26) -6	34) -4
4) $\frac{34}{5}$	11) 0	19) 7	27) 10	35) 200
5) $\frac{9}{13}$	12) -1	20) -5	28) 3	36) 5
6) $-\frac{7}{2}$	13) 3	21) 11	29) -17	37) -2
7) 5	14) 2	22) 4	30) 6	
	15) 2	23) 3	31) 7	

Find the Slope, $x-$ intercept and $y-$intercept

1) $y = -1, x = -2$
2) $y = -3, x = \frac{3}{2}$
3) $y = -\frac{1}{3}, x = -\frac{1}{3}$

4) $y = 1, x = -\frac{2}{5}$
5) $y = 5, x = -2$
6) $y = 1, x = 2$
7) $y = \frac{1}{2}, x = 2$

8) $y = \frac{9}{4}, x = \frac{9}{2}$
9) $y = \frac{7}{3}, x = -\frac{7}{2}$

Write an equation from a graph

1) $y = -\frac{3}{2}x - 3$
2) $y = 3x - 13$

3) $y = -7x + 4$
4) $y = \frac{1}{2}x + 7$

5) $y = -2x + \frac{1}{2}$
6) $y = 4x$

Slope–intercept form

1) $y = \frac{1}{4}x - 4$
2) $y = \frac{2}{3}x - 2$
3) $y = \frac{3}{10}x + 1$
4) $y = -2x + 2$
5) $y = -2x + 4$

6) $y = \frac{1}{3}x - \frac{1}{9}$
7) $y = -x + 1$
8) $y = 2x - 2$
9) $y = 3x - 2$
10) $y = \frac{5}{x}x - \frac{5}{4}$
11) $y = -x + 2$

12) $y = \frac{1}{3}x + 2$
13) $l = 34 - \frac{1}{2}d, 16\ days$
14) $28
15) 90

Point–slope form

1) $m = 3 , (-3,0)$

2) $m = 3, \left(\frac{2}{3}, 0\right)$

3) $m = 4, (-3,-9)$

4) $m = \frac{2}{3}, (0,-1)$

5) $m = 4, (-2,-3)$

6) $m = \frac{3}{2}, (0,-2)$

7) $m = 4, \left(\frac{1}{2}, 1\right)$

8) $m = \frac{2}{3}, \left(0, \frac{4}{3}\right)$

9) $m = 3, (1,-1)$

10) $m = 1, \left(-\frac{10}{4}, 2\right)$

11) $m = 32, (-1,-1)$

12) $m = 5, (-1,-2)$

13) $y = \frac{1}{2}x + 1$

14) $y = 3x - 5$

15) $y = -2x + 4$

16) $y = 3x - 11$

17) $y = -\frac{1}{2}x - 4$

18) $y = 3x - \frac{11}{4}$

19) $y = -\frac{3}{4}x - \frac{3}{2}$

20) $y = 2x + \frac{19}{14}$

21) $y = 5x + 2$

22) $y = \frac{4}{5}x + \frac{17}{5}$

23) $y = 4x + \frac{25}{6}$

24) $y = \frac{1}{5}x - 1$

25) $y = 10x - 37$

26) $y = -x - 11$

27) $y = -\frac{2}{3}x - 4$

28) $y = -4x + 5$

29) $y = -4x - 10$

30) $y = \frac{1}{2}x + \frac{1}{2}$

31) $y = \frac{7}{3}x + \frac{34}{3}$

32) $y = \frac{1}{2}x + 1$

33) $y = 2x - 7$

34) $y = -x$

35) $y = -2x - 2$

36) $y = 4x - 19$

37) $y = 3x - 5$

Equations of horizontal and vertical lines

1) $y = 0$ (it is on x axes)

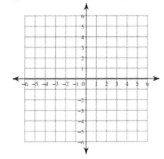

2) $y = 2$

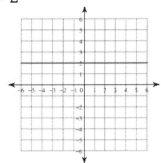

3) $x = -4$

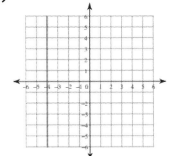

4) $x = 3$

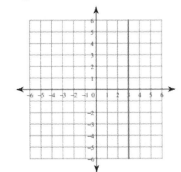

Equation of parallel or perpendicular lines

1) $y = \frac{3}{2}x + 6$

2) $y = -\frac{1}{3}x + 7$

3) $y = \frac{1}{3}x - 3$

4) $y = -2x$

5) $y = -\frac{1}{2}x + \frac{7}{2}$

6) $y = -\frac{1}{2}x + \frac{13}{2}$

7) $y = -x + 5$

8) $y = 3x - 4$

9) $y = x + 6$

10) $y = x + 5$

11) $y = -\frac{1}{3}x + \frac{1}{3}$

12) $y = \frac{1}{2}x - 7$

13) $y = -x$

14) $y = x + 6$

15) $y = \frac{1}{3}x - \frac{5}{3}$

16) $y = -\frac{1}{3}x + \frac{7}{3}$

17) $y = -2x - 6$

18) $y = \frac{1}{5}x + \frac{11}{5}$

19) $Y = 8x, \$32$

Chapter 9:

Monomials and Polynomials

Topics that you'll learn in this part:

- ✓ Classifying Polynomials
- ✓ Writing Polynomials in Standard Form
- ✓ Simplifying Polynomials
- ✓ Add and Subtract Monomials
- ✓ Multiplying Monomials
- ✓ Multiplying and Dividing Monomials
- ✓ GCF of Monomials
- ✓ Powers of Monomials
- ✓ Multiplying a Polynomial and a Monomial
- ✓ Multiplying Binomials
- ✓ Factoring Trinomials

Writing Polynomials in Standard Form

✎ *Write each polynomial in standard form.*

1) $3x^2 - 4x^3 + 1 =$

2) $7x - x^3 + 5x^2 =$

3) $15x + x^3 =$

4) $2(x^2 + 1) + x^4 =$

5) $(x - 1)x + 1) =$

6) $x(3x + 7) - x^4 =$

7) $15x - 4x^2 - 7x + 3 =$

8) $3(x - 2) - x^3 =$

9) $6x(x - 4) + 4x^2 + 1 =$

10) $3x^2 - 4x - 2(x^2 + 1) =$

11) $4x^3 + 2x - 5x^5 =$

12) $2 - 4x - 2(x^2 + 1) =$

13) $3x + (x + 1)(x + 1) =$

14) $4x - 5x^3 + 4 =$

15) $14y - 3y^2 + 2y =$

16) $4m(m^2 - 1) + 3m^4 =$

17) $2x - 4x^2 - 7x - 3x =$

18) $7x^3 + \frac{x^3 + x^2}{x^2} =$

19) $\frac{4N^4 + 4N}{2N} + N^2 =$

20) $17x^2 - 4x^5 + x^{10} =$

21) $-3x^5 + 4x - 9x^2 =$

22) $2x(x + 1) + \frac{3x + x^2}{x} =$

23) $17x - 4x^3 + 5x^2 + 1 =$

24) $(-3)\frac{x^2 - 9x + 15x^3}{3x} + x^3 =$

25) $14x^5 + \frac{x^5 + x^4}{2x^2} =$

26) $12x - 4 + 4x^3 + x^2 =$

27) $4x^3 + 7x^2 + 28x^5 =$

28) $34x^4 - 2x + 7x^2 =$

29) $2x^2(x^2 + 4x) + x =$

30) $-3x^2 + 4x - 7x^3 =$

31) $25x\left(\frac{1}{5}x^2 - \frac{x}{2}\right) =$

32) $x^2 + 4x^5 + x^3 =$

33) $2x^2 - 3x - 7x^2 - x =$

34) $2x^2 - 4x^4 + x^2 =$

35) $-3x + 7x^2 - x(x + 1) =$

36) $5x - x^2 + x^5 + x^3 =$

37) $4 + 2x - x^2 =$

38) $2z - 3 + z^3 =$

39) $p^6 - 2 + 3p^3 =$

40) $2y - 2y^6 + y^4 =$

41) $9x + x^2 - 7 =$

42) $2x + 1 =$

43) $3z^3 + 5 =$

44) $2 - 3q + q^2$

Simplifying Polynomials

✎*Simplify each expression.*

1) $(-5)(4m^2 - 5m - 8)$

2) $2d(d^5 - 7d^3 + 4)$

3) $7rs(4r^2 + 9s^3 - 7rs)$

4) $8x^4(6x - 8x^3 + 7)$

5) $(y + 3)(y + 5)$

6) $(2x + 4)(x + 9)$

7) $(4b - 3)(4b + 3)$

8) $(n + 4m)(2n - 3m)$

9) $(x + 4)(6x^2 + 2x - 8)$

10) $(4z + 6)(4z + 6)$

11) $(x - 2)(9 - 5x)$

12) $(4b - 3)(4b - 3)$

13) $(3x^2 - 2x)(7x - 8x^2 - 9)$

✎*Solve.*

14) Find the perimeter of the triangle pictured.

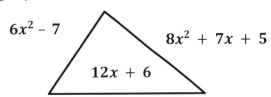

15) Find the area of the rectangles pictured.

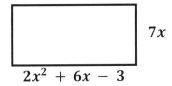

16) A triangle has sides of length $3x + 4y$, $5y + 6 + 2x$, and $7 + 8x$. What is the perimeter of the triangle?

17) Triangle has a perimeter $10x^2 - 3xy - 6y^2$. If two sides are known to be $2x^2 + 2xy$ and $7x^2 + 3y^2$, then what is the length of the third unknown side?

Add and Subtract monomials

✎ *Find each sum and difference.*

1) $3x^3y - 12x^3y =$

2) $10(3uv - u) + 5u =$

3) $12x^2z - z(5x^2 - z) =$

4) $3x^2(z + y) - 2x^2z =$

5) $14(x^2yz^2 - x) + x^2yz^2 + 12x =$

6) $6\frac{x^2}{y} - 4\frac{x^2}{y} =$

7) $3\left(x^2 + \frac{1}{y}\right) - x^2 + \frac{2}{y} =$

8) $3x^2z + (x^2)(2z) =$

9) $3\frac{z}{y}x^2 + 2x^2\left(1 + \frac{z}{y}\right) - x^2 =$

10) $3uvw - 15uvw =$

11) $12ux^2 - 14ux^2 =$

12) $3x(x^2 + y) + x^3 - 4xy =$

13) $3y^2zx^2 + 17x^2(zy^2 + 1) =$

14) $10m^6 + 12m^6 - 14m^6 =$

15) $32e^{-i\omega t} - 18e^{-i\omega t} =$

16) $15lq - 5lq + lq =$

17) $\frac{xyz}{2} + \frac{3}{2}xyz =$

18) $95\,lqr - 39lqr =$

19) $33\frac{z^3x}{y} - 19\frac{z^3x}{y} =$

20) $7(x^2z - y) + x^2z =$

21) $x^2zy - 2x^2(1 - zy) + 2x^2 =$

22) $33(x^2 + rs) - 30x^2 - 45rs =$

23) $12z^3x - 18z^3x =$

24) $x^2(yz) + 12x^2(yz) =$

25) $4xy - 15xy =$

26) $-2x^2y + x^2y - 3x^2y =$

27) $3\frac{x^2}{z} + 10\frac{x^2}{z} - 2\frac{x^2}{z} =$

28) $4yzu - 12yzu =$

29) $12ut - 14ut - 33ut =$

30) $15frq + 3frq =$

31) $12(x - yz) + 12x - 9yz =$

32) $10(x^2 - 2y) + 18y =$

33) $3\frac{xyz}{t} + 4\frac{xyz}{t} =$

34) $33\left(t^2e^{-i\omega t}\right) - \left(40t^2e^{-i\omega t}\right) =$

35) $\frac{t^3x}{z} + 4\left(\frac{t^3x}{z} - x\right) + 3x =$

36) $5wt - 12wt - 33wt =$

37) $2x + \frac{(x+1)^2}{x+1} =$

38) $3x^3 - 2x - 4x^3 + x =$

39) $2z^2 - 4z - 3z^2 =$

40) $\frac{(3x+1)(3x-1)}{3x-1} + x =$

41) $9r - 3r^2 - 8r =$

42) $3t(t + 1) - 3t =$

Multiplying Monomials

✎ *Simplify each expression.*

1) $(2x)(2x)^3 =$

2) $(2n^5)(n^2)^2 =$

3) $\left(\dfrac{x^2}{2}\right)^5 (3x) =$

4) $\left(\dfrac{2b}{3}\right)^4 (3b) =$

5) $-2x \left(\dfrac{1}{2x^2}\right)^4 =$

6) $(x\left(\dfrac{1}{2}x\right)^2)^3 =$

7) $5x^2 z(2z) =$

8) $12xyz(x^2 z) =$

9) $x^2 y(12xz) =$

10) $3x^2 z^3 (2yzx) =$

11) $7(x^2 zt)(t^2 zx) =$

12) $(-2u^3 vw)(4vw) =$

13) $(-5)(mn^3)(3nm^2)(mn) =$

14) $2(x^2 y)(yz)(zxy) =$

15) $3v^2 (9uw)(vw)^5 =$

16) $6(x^5)(xz^4)(zxy) =$

17) $(3c^3 b)(b^2 a)(cb) =$

18) $14x(3xz)(2yz) =$

19) $x^2 (3yzx)(z^3 xy) =$

20) $-5z^4 (y^5 z)(3xz) =$

21) $3(u^3 v)(uv^3)(uvw)(wv) =$

22) $2\left(e^{-i\omega t}xt\right)\left(te^{-i\omega t}x\right) =$

23) $3(m^3 n^2)(mn)(2n^3) =$

24) $(x^2 z)(z^3 xy)(yx) =$

25) $(g^2 l)(l^2 g)(gl) =$

26) $-2(x^2 z)(3yx)(4zxy) =$

27) $(2x^5)(3xy^2)(zx) =$

28) $(p^3 qt)(2qp)(t^2 q) =$

29) $7(m^4 nq)(2mn)(qmn^2) =$

30) $(12pt)(3p)(t^2 p) =$

31) $(pls)(2p^2 s)(s^3 pl) =$

32) $\left(\dfrac{z^5}{t}\right)\left(3\dfrac{z^5}{t}\right)(-2)\left(\dfrac{z^5}{t}\right) =$

33) $(33x^2)(xy)(zxy) =$

34) $\left(2\left(\dfrac{z}{t}\right)^3\right)\left(4\dfrac{z^5}{t}\right)\left(\dfrac{z^5}{t}\right)^6 =$

35) $\left(\dfrac{2x}{z}\right)^5 \left(\dfrac{2x}{z}\right)\left(\dfrac{2x}{z}\right)^3 =$

36) $(\dfrac{m}{n^2})(2\left(\dfrac{m}{n^2}\right)^3) =$

37) $x^2(zy)(3y) =$

38) $4\left(\dfrac{x^2}{zy}\right)^2 \left(4\left(\dfrac{x^2}{zy}\right)\right) =$

39) $(\dfrac{\sqrt{a^2+b^2}}{b})(3\left(\dfrac{\sqrt{a^2+b^2}}{b}\right)^3) =$

40) $\left(3\left(\dfrac{t^4}{g}\right)\right)\left(2\left(\dfrac{t^4}{g}\right)^{10}\right) =$

Multiplying and Dividing Monomials

✎ *Simplify.*

1) $\dfrac{3x^2yz^5}{xyz} =$

2) $\dfrac{25x(2xz^5)}{25x^2z^3} =$

3) $2\left(\dfrac{x^2m^5n^4}{x^3mn^4}\right)(2xn) =$

4) $3\dfrac{q}{r}\left(\dfrac{q^2r^5}{qr}\right) =$

5) $\dfrac{(3xy^3)(4xyz^3)}{12xyz} =$

6) $m^4(n^2)\left(\dfrac{5n^2}{m^3n^4}\right) =$

7) $\dfrac{3x(2xy)(3xz)}{9x^2} =$

8) $\left(\dfrac{3z^5x^2}{3z^3y}\right)\left(\dfrac{y}{z^3}\right) =$

9) $(3x^2y^2z^2)\left(\dfrac{2x}{x^2yz^2}\right) =$

10) $\left(\dfrac{e^{-i\omega t}}{t}\right)\left(\dfrac{t^3}{e^{-i\omega t}}\right) =$

11) $(3u^3v^2w)\left(\dfrac{1}{uvw^2}\right) =$

12) $2(mnl)(m^2nl^3)\left(\dfrac{1}{m^2l}\right) =$

13) $23(a^2b)\left(\dfrac{2ab}{b^2}\right) =$

14) $6(x^2zt)(xz^2t) =$

15) $\dfrac{3(ab)(c^2b)(abc)}{c^4a^3b} =$

16) $3x^2\left(\dfrac{(xz^3y)(2yz)}{x^2}\right)z^3 =$

17) $4x(12x^2)(z^4)\left(\dfrac{1}{z^3x^2}\right) =$

18) $\dfrac{(ab)(ab)^2(-2(ab)^5)}{(ab)^6} =$

19) $\left(\dfrac{x(w)^{2t}}{x(w)^t}\right)2xt =$

20) $2xt(t^5x)(2t^2) =$

21) $\left(\dfrac{(3a)(3b)(c^2ab)}{3(a^2bc^2)}\right) =$

22) $(-2x^2y)\left(\dfrac{1}{2zyx}\right) =$

23) $\dfrac{\left(x\sqrt{z}\right)^5(2xz)\left(x\sqrt{z}\right)}{2\left(x\sqrt{z}\right)^3} =$

24) $3(x^2y^3)\left(\dfrac{2xy}{y^5zx^2}\right) =$

25) $(3uv^3)\left(\dfrac{uvw}{u^2vw}\right) =$

26) $(m^4n^6)(\dfrac{3nm(2n^2)}{3m^2n^3} =$

27) $x^2e^{3(i\omega t)}(\dfrac{15t}{e^{2(i\omega t)}x}) =$

28) $33xyz(2x^2zy) =$

29) $e^3hq\left(\dfrac{3hq}{6eq^2}\right) =$

30) $2(x^2z)(3zy)(zy) =$

31) $8z\left(\dfrac{2z^2-z^5}{8z^3}\right) =$

32) $\left(\dfrac{6q^4+3q^3}{3q}\right)\left(\dfrac{1}{q^2}\right) =$

33) $\left(\dfrac{1}{x^2-2x}\right)\left(\dfrac{10x^2-20x}{5}\right) =$

34) $(2x^2)\left(\dfrac{5}{x}\right) =$

GCF of Monomials

✍ *Find the GCF of each set of monomials.*

1) $6x^2z, 2xy$

2) $2x^2y^5z, 14yz$

3) $3u^3vw^4, 6vw$

4) $10x^2yz, 5y^2x$

5) $3x^2z^4, \left(\frac{x^2z^2}{x^2z}\right)$

6) $9uv^5w, 3uw$

7) $4trq^5, \left(\frac{t^3rq}{trq}\right)$

8) $\left(\frac{12x^2z^4y}{x^2zy}\right), -2xzy$

9) $11n^4pm^5, 11pmn^2$

10) $14xz^4ty^5, \left(\frac{7x^2yt^3}{xt}\right)$

11) $6x^2y^3, xyz, 3x^2$

12) $15d^3eh^3, 5edh, 7deh^2$

13) $\left(\frac{2x^2y^5z}{yz}\right), 3xz, 4x^2y$

14) $33x^5zy^5, 22x^2y$

15) $\left(\frac{(-2xyz)(x^2)}{3x^3z}\right), 2xzy$

16) $21x^2mn, 35nx$

17) $3a(b^2ac), a^2c, 3ab$

18) $\left(\frac{m^4n^2p}{np}\right), 2m(nm)$

19) $15x^2\left(\frac{3x^2yz}{xz}\right), 5y^5zx^2$

20) $e^5hq, \left(\frac{3e^6h^4q}{e^4hq}\right)$

21) $\left(\frac{2x^2(4z^4x^2y)}{4xz^2y}\right), 32x^2yz$

22) $14mp^5t^4, 7m^6t^3p^2$

23) $\left(\frac{(-2mn)(n^4m^3)}{n^5m}\right), -n^5m^7$

24) $(x^2)(-7yz^5x^2), 2x^2y$

25) $25\left(\frac{x^2yz^4}{15yz}\right), 3x^2yz^8$

26) $(-3ab)(3bc), 3acb^2$

27) $\left(\frac{(ab)(bc)(ca)}{2ba^2}\right), 8a^3b^6c$

28) $9r^3q^5s^2, \left(\frac{(rsq^2)(3sq)}{3srq}\right)$

29) $2mny^3t, 4mty$

30) $3(abc)(2ca), 20a^2cb$

31) $2\frac{(x^2y^5z^4)}{2xz}, 2xy$

32) $3xy(2xyz), x^2z(yx)$

33) $25azx(3xz), 25a^3zx^2$

34) $33x^2 + 11x, 11x^2 + 22x$

35) $\frac{5}{(x-1)(x+3)}, \frac{-5}{x-1}$

36) $\frac{2x^5+x^2}{x}, x^2$

37) $2z^5 + z, z^3$

38) $2x(1-y), (x-xy)$

Powers of monomials

✎ *Simplify.*

1) $\left(\frac{1}{2x}\right)\left(\frac{2x}{3}\right)^3 =$

2) $\left(\frac{3xy}{3z}\right)^2 (2z) =$

3) $\left(\frac{x^2 zt}{2z^3}\right)^3 (8z^9) =$

4) $\left(\frac{(2x)^2}{yz}\right)^3 =$

5) $\left(\frac{(2m+1)}{3m^2}\right)^2 =$

6) $(zt^{10}b)^2(3z) =$

7) $(2x^2 yz)^3 =$

8) $3(2mn^2)^4 =$

9) $(2x^2 z^4 y)^2 =$

10) $4(y^3 xz)^5 =$

11) $(x^2 y^2 z^4)^3 =$

12) $(-2x^{ab} y^3)^3 =$

13) $\left(\frac{x^2 y}{z}\right)^{ab} =$

14) $(-2a^6 b^2 c^4)^{5x} =$

15) $(x^2 y^{2ab} z^{2b})^3 =$

16) $\left(\frac{x^2 yz^5}{t}\right)^6 =$

17) $\left(\frac{(3x^2 y^3 z)}{2zy}\right)^2 =$

18) $(4x^2 z^4)^{ab} =$

19) $(m^{10} n^6 r)^3 =$

20) $(2yx^2 z)^2 =$

21) $(x^2 y^2 z^3)^{2t} =$

22) $(3x^2 yz^3)^5 =$

23) $\left(\frac{(2xyz^2)^4}{2xy}\right)^2 =$

24) $\left(\frac{(x^2 yz^3)^3}{(xz)^2}\right)^2 =$

25) $\frac{(2xy)^3}{(x^2 yz^4)^b} =$

26) $(x^2 z)^2 (2xy)^4 =$

27) $3(2x^2 z)^5 =$

28) $(a^4 bc^5)^{12} =$

29) $(10^x 12^y 5^z)^m =$

30) $(\propto^5 \beta^6 \gamma^8)^2 =$

31) $\left(\frac{(x^2 y)^2 (2zy)^2}{(xyz)^a}\right)^2 =$

32) $(2xy^5 z^4 x^2)^3 =$

33) $\left(\frac{x^2 yz^2}{(xy)^a}\right)^b =$

34) $(t^6 r^5 s^6)^{(a+b)} =$

35) $2(x^2 yx^4)^3 =$

36) $(abc^2)^2 (a^2)^4 =$

37) $2(2x)^2 (x^2 yz)^2 =$

38) $\left(\frac{(xy^3 z^2)^2}{x^2 (2yz)^3}\right) =$

39) $(2x)^2 (x^6 z^3)^{\frac{1}{3}} =$

40) $(t^2 x^2 y^5)^{3ab} =$

Multiplying a Polynomial and a Monomial

✎ *Find each product.*

1) $(2xy)\left(\frac{1}{2x+1}\right) =$

2) $\left(\frac{1}{3z+4}\right)\left(\frac{2xy+1}{3}\right) =$

3) $(-2rq)(3q - 3r + 1) =$

4) $\frac{3ca^3}{2}\left(1 + \frac{2}{ca}\right) =$

5) $3x(2x + 1) =$

6) $3b(b^2 - 1) =$

7) $2x(1 - 2x) =$

8) $\frac{x}{3}(3x^2 - 6y^3) =$

9) $yx^2(z^2 + xy) =$

10) $2x^4(z^2 - y) =$

11) $3ab(a^2 - b^2) =$

12) $z^2 t\left(3ztx - \frac{2}{zt}\right) =$

13) $\frac{x}{y}\left(2x^2 + 3y - \frac{y}{x}\right) =$

14) $3ac(a^2 - 2ab + b^2) =$

15) $(-b)\left(\frac{3x}{2} + \frac{2x}{b}\right) =$

16) $a^b(x^2 - 2x + 4) =$

17) $(-2xy)(c - b + a) =$

18) $\rho\left(\frac{l}{s} - 2ls - s^2\right) =$

19) $2x^2yz(1 - 4x - 2y) =$

20) $y^3xz\left(25x - \frac{1}{y^3}\right) =$

21) $3uv(u^2 + 2uv + v^2) =$

22) $\left(-2\frac{x}{yz}\right)\left(\frac{2yz^2}{3x} - 2yz - xyz\right) =$

23) $3b^2(b^2 - 4ac) =$

24) $\frac{-b}{2a}(1 - b^2 - ac) =$

25) $5xy(3zx - xy + 2x^2) =$

26) $x^2y(3 - z) =$

27) $(2x + 2y - z)(-2y) =$

28) $2a(-x^2 - 2y^3 + xy) =$

29) $\frac{3xz}{y^3}\left(1 - \frac{2y^3}{xz}\right) =$

30) $7v(2ut - 2vt) =$

31) $4u^4(1 - 2v + 5w) =$

32) $\frac{x^2}{3z}\left(z^2 + 2z - \frac{2}{x^2}\right) =$

33) $6mz\left(\frac{12+m}{3z}\right) =$

34) $e^{2x}(1 - 3xz + 4y) =$

35) $\frac{2x^2}{z}(3 + 2z - y) =$

36) $(-x)^2(x^2 + 2x - 1) =$

37) $2v^2w\left(\frac{1-3u+5vw}{vw} - 1\right) =$

38) $2x^0(3x + 4z - 2zxy) =$

39) $4x(2x - 1) =$

40) $18x^2\left(\frac{1}{3x^2}\right) =$

Multiplying Binomials

✎ *Simplify each expression.*

1) $(x-5)(x+4) =$

2) $(x-6)(x-3) =$

3) $(x+4)(x+7) =$

4) $(x+3)(x-7) =$

5) $(3x-5)(2x+8) =$

6) $(11x-7)(5x+3) =$

7) $(4x-9)(9x+4) =$

8) $(x-2)(x+2) =$

9) $(x-2)(x-2) =$

10) $(x+4)(x-5) =$

11) $(3x-7)(x+3) =$

12) $(x-5)(4x+9) =$

13) $(3x+7)(8x-1) =$

14) $(x-1)(x+4) =$

15) $(10x+7)(x-11) =$

16) $(4x^2+1)(3-x) =$

✎ *Find the area of each shape.*

17)

x + 3

x + 3

19)

$x + 6$

$x + 3$

18)

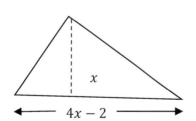

x

$4x - 2$

20)

$2x + 7$

x − 2

Factoring Trinomials

✎*Factor each trinomial.*

1) $x^2 + 8x + 15 =$

2) $x^2 - 5x + 6 =$

3) $x^2 + 6x + 8 =$

4) $x^2 - 6x + 8 =$

5) $x^2 - 8x + 16 =$

6) $x^2 - 7x + 12 =$

7) $x^2 + 11x + 18 =$

8) $x^2 + 2x - 24 =$

9) $x^2 + 4x - 12 =$

10) $x^2 - 10x + 9 =$

11) $x^2 + 5x - 14 =$

12) $x^2 - 6x - 27 =$

13) $x^2 - 11x - 42 =$

14) $x^2 + 22x + 121 =$

15) $6x^2 + x - 12 =$

16) $x^2 - 17x + 30 =$

17) $3x^2 + 11x - 4 =$

18) $10x^2 + 33x - 7 =$

19) $x^2 + 24x + 144 =$

20) $8x^2 + 10x - 3 =$

✎*Solve.*

21) A certain company's main source of income is a mobile app. The company's annual profit (in millions of dollars) as a function of the app's price (in dollars) is modeled by $P(x) = -2(x - 3)(x - 11)$. Which app prices will result in $0 annual profit?

22) A rectangular plot is 6 meters longer than it is wide. The area of the plot is 16 square meters. Find the length and width of the plot.

23) The combined area of two squares is 20 square centimeters. Each side of one square is twice as long as a side of the other square. Find the lengths of the sides of each square.

Answers of Worksheets

Writing Polynomials in Standard Form

1) $-4x^3 + 3x^2 + 1$

2) $-x^3 + 5x^2 + 7x$

3) $x^3 + 15$

4) $x^4 + 2x^2 + 2$

5) $x^2 - 1$

6) $-x^4 + 3x^2 + 7x$

7) $-4x^2 + 8x + 3$

8) $-x^3 + 3x - 6$

9) $10x^2 - 24x + 1$

10) $x^2 - 4x - 2$

11) $-5x^5 + 4x^3 + 2x$

12) $-2x^2 - 4x$

13) $x^2 + 5x + 1$

14) $-5x^3 + 4x + 4$

15) $-3y^2 + 16y$

16) $3m^4 + 4m^3 - 4m$

17) $-4x^2 - 8x$

18) $7x^3 + x + 1$

19) $2N^3 + N^2 + 2$

20) $x^{10} - 4x^5 + 17x^2$

21) $-3x^5 - 9x^2 + 4x$

22) $2x^2 + 3x + 3$

23) $-4x^3 + 5x^2 + 17x + 1$

24) $x^3 - 15x^2 - x + 9$

25) $14x^5 + \frac{1}{2}x^3 + \frac{1}{2}x^2$

26) $4x^3 + x^2 + 12x - 4$

27) $28x^5 + 4x^3 + 7x^2$

28) $34x^4 + 7x^2 - 2x$

29) $2x^4 + 8x^3 + x$

30) $-7x^3 - 3x^2 + 4x$

31) $5x^3 - \frac{25}{2}x^2$

32) $4x^5 + x^3 + x^2$

33) $-5x^2 - 4x$

34) $-4x^4 + 3x^2$

35) $6x^2 - 4x$

36) $x^5 + x^3 - x^2 + 5x$

37) $-x^2 + 2x + 4$

38) $z^3 + 2z - 3$

39) $p^6 + 3p^3 - 2$

40) $-2y^6 + y^4 + 2y$

41) $x^2 + 9x - 7$

42) $2x + 1$

43) $3z^3 + 5$

44) $q^2 - 3q + 2$

Simplifying Polynomials

1) $-20m^2 + 25m + 40$

2) $2d^6 - 14d^4 + 8d$

3) $28r^3s + 63rs^4 - 49r^2s^2$

4) $-64x^7 + 48x^5 + 56x^4$

5) $y^2 + 8y + 15$

6) $2x^2 + 22x + 36$

7) $16b^2 - 9$

8) $2n^2 - 12m^2 + 5mn$

9) $6x^3 + 26x^2 - 32$

10) $16z^2 + 48z + 36$

11) $-5x^2 + 19x - 18$

12) $16b^2 - 24b + 9$

13) $-24x^4 + 37x^3 - 41x^2 - 18x$

14) $14x^2 + 19x - 1$

15) $14x^3 + 42x^2$

16) $13x + 9y + 13$

17) $x^2 - 5xy - 9y^2$

Add and Subtract Monomials

1) $-9x^3y$

2) $(30uv - 5u)$

3) $7x^2z + z^2$

4) $3x^2y + x^2z$

5) $15x^2yz^2 - 2x$

6) $2\frac{x^2}{y}$

7) $2x^2 + \frac{1}{y}$

8) $5x^2z$

9) $5\frac{z}{y}x^2 + x^2$

10) $-12uvw$

11) $-2ux^2$

12) $4x^3 - xy$

13) $20y^2zx^2 + 17x^2$

14) $8m^6$

15) $14e^{-i\omega t}$

16) $11lq$

17) $2xyz$

18) $56\,lqr$

19) $14\frac{z^3x}{y}$

20) $8x^2z - 7y$

21) $3x^2zy$

22) $3x^2 - 12rs$

23) $-6z^3x$

24) $13x^2yx$

25) $-11xy$

26) $-4x^2y$

27) $11\frac{x^2}{z}$

28) $-8yzu$

29) $-35ut$

30) $18frq$

31) $24x - 21yz$

32) $10x^2 - 2y$

33) $7\frac{xyz}{t}$

34) $-7\left(t^2e^{-i\omega t}\right)$

35) $5\frac{t^3x}{z} - x$

36) $-40wt$

37) $3x + 1$

38) $-x^3 - x$

39) $-z^2 - 4z$

40) $4x + 1$

41) $-3r^2 + r$

42) $3t^2$

Multiplying Monomials

1) $(2x)^4$

2) $2n^9$

3) $\frac{3x^{11}}{32}$

4) $\frac{16b^5}{27}$

5) $\frac{-1}{8x^7}$

6) $\frac{x^9}{64}$

7) $10x^2z^2$

8) $12x^3yz^2$

9) $12x^3yz$

10) $6x^3z^4y$

11) $7(x^3z^2t^3)$

12) $(-8u^3v^2w^2)$

13) $(-15)(m^4n^5)$

14) $2(x^3y^3z^2)$

15) $27v^7uw^6$

16) $6(x^7z^5y)$

17) $(3ac^4b^4)$

18) $84x^2yz^2$

19) $3x^4y^2z^4$

20) $-15xy^5z^6$

21) $3(u^5v^6w^2)$

22) $2(e^{-2i\omega t}x^2t)$

23) $6(m^4n^6)$

24) $(x^4z^4y^2)$

25) (g^4l^4)

26) $-24(x^4y^2z^2)$

27) $(6x^7y^2z)$

28) $(2p^4q^3t^3)$

29) $14(m^6n^4q^2)$

30) $(36p^3t^3)$

31) $2(p^4l^2s^5)$

32) $(-6)\frac{z^{15}}{t^3}$

33) $(33x^4y^2z)$

34) $8\frac{z^{38}}{t^{10}}$

35) $\frac{512x^9}{z^9}$

36) $2\left(\frac{m}{n^2}\right)^4$

37) $3x^2y^2z$

38) $16\left(\frac{x^2}{zy}\right)^3$

39) $3\left(\frac{\sqrt{a^2+b^2}}{b}\right)^4$

40) $6\left(\frac{t^4}{g}\right)^{11}$

Multiplying and Dividing Monomials

1) $3xz^4$

2) $2z^2$

3) $4m^4n$

4) $3q^2r^3$

5) xy^3z^2

6) $5m$

7) $2xyz$

8) $\frac{x^2}{z}$

9) $6xy$

10) t^2

11) $\left(\frac{3u^2v}{w}\right)$

12) $2(mn^2l^3)$

13) $46a^3$

14) $6(x^2z^3t^2)$

15) $\frac{3b^2}{ca}$

16) $6z^7xy^2$

17) $48xz$

18) $-2(ab)^2$

19) $2xwt$

20) $4x^2t^8$

21) $3b$

22) $\left(-\frac{x}{z}\right)$

23) $xz\left(x\sqrt{z}\right)^3$

24) $\frac{6x}{yz}$

25) $3v^3$

26) $2m^3n^6$

27) $15txe^{(i\omega t)}$

28) $66x^3y^2z^2$

29) $\frac{1}{2}e^2h^2$

30) $6(x^2z^3y^2)$

31) $2-z^3$

32) $2q+1$

33) 2

34) $10x$

GCF of monomials

1) $2x$

2) $2yz$

3) $3vw$

4) $5xy$

5) z

6) $3uw$

7) t

8) $2z$

9) $11pmn^2$

10) $7xt$

11) x

12) deh

13) x

14) $11x^2y$

15) $2y$

16) xn

17) a

18) m^2n

19) $5x^2y$

20) e^2h

21) $2x^2z$

22) $7mp^2t^3$

23) $-m^3$

24) x^2y

25) x^2z^3

26) $3acb^2$

27) bc

28) q^2s

29) $2mty$

30) $2a^2cb$

31) $2xy$

32) x^2yz

33) $25azx^2$

34) $11x$

35) $\frac{5}{x-1}$

36) x

37) z

38) $x(1-y)$

Powers of monomials

1) $\frac{4x^2}{27}$

2) $\frac{2x^2y^2}{z}$

3) $x^6z^3t^3$

4) $\frac{64x^6}{y^3z^3}$

5) $\frac{(2m+1)^2}{9m^4}$

6) $3z^3t^{20}b^2$

7) $8x^6y^3z^3$

8) $48m^4n^8$

9) $4x^4z^8y^2$

10) $4y^{15}x^5z^5$

11) $x^6y^6z^{12}$

12) $-8x^{3ab}y^9$

13) $\frac{x^{2ab}y^{ab}}{z^{ab}}$

14) $(-2)^{5x}a^{30x}b^{10x}c^{20x}$

15) $x^6y^{6ab}z^{6b}$

16) $\frac{x^{12}y^6z^{30}}{t^6}$

17) $\frac{9x^4y^6z^2}{4z^2y^2}$

18) $4^{ab}x^{2ab}z^{4ab}$

19) $m^{30}n^{18}r^3$

20) $4y^2x^4z^2$

21) $x^{4t}y^{4t}z^{6t}$

22) $243x^{10}y^5z^{15}$

23) $\frac{256x^8y^8z^{16}}{4x^2y^2}$

24) $\frac{x^{12}y^6z^{18}}{x^4z^4}$

25) $\frac{8x^3y^3}{x^{2b}y^bz^{4b}}$

26) $16x^8z^2y^4$

27) $96x^{10}z^5$

28) $a^{48}b^{12}c^{60}$

29) $10^{mx}12^{my}5^{mz}$

30) $\propto^{10}\beta^{12}\gamma^{16}$

31) $\frac{16x^8y^8z^4}{x^{2a}y^{2a}z^{2a}}$

32) $8x^9y^{15}z^{12}$

33) $\frac{x^{2b}y^bz^{2b}}{x^{ab}y^{ab}}$

34) $t^{6(a+b)}r^{5(a+b)}s^{6(a+b)}$

35) $2x^6y^3x^{12}$

36) $a^{10}b^2c^4$

37) $8x^6y^2z^2$

38) $\frac{x^2y^6z^4}{8x^2y^3z^3}$

39) $4x^4z$

40) $t^{6ab}x^{6ab}y^{15ab}$

Multiplying a Polynomial and a Monomial

1) $\frac{2xy}{2x+1}$

2) $\frac{2xy+1}{9z+12}$

3) $-6rq^2 + 6r^2q - 2rq$

4) $\frac{3ca^3}{2} + 3a^2$

5) $6x^2 + 3x$

6) $3b^3 - 3b$

7) $2x - 4x^2$

8) $x^3 - 2xy^3$

9) $yx^2z^2 + x^3y^2$

10) $2x^4z^2 - 2x^4y$

11) $3a^3b - 3ab^3$

12) $3z^3t^2x - 2z$

13) $\frac{2x^3}{y} + 3x - 1$

14) $3ca^3 - 6a^2bc + 3acb^2$

15) $-\frac{3bx}{2} - 2x$

16) $x^2a^b - 2xa^b + 4a^b$

17) $-2xyc + 2xyb - 2xya$

18) $\frac{\rho l}{s} - 2\rho ls - \rho s^2$

19) $(2x^2yz - 82x^3yz - 4x^2y^2z)$

20) $25y^3x^2z - xz$

21) $3u^3v + 6u^2v^2 + 3uv^3$

22) $\frac{-4z}{3} + 4x + 2x^2$

23) $3b^4 - 12ab^2c$

24) $\frac{-b}{2a} + \frac{b^3}{2a} + \frac{bc}{2}$

25) $15x^2yz - 5x^2y^2 + 10x^3y$

26) $3x^2y - x^2yz$

27) $-4xy - 4y^2 + 2yz$

28) $-2ax^2 - 4ay^3 + 2axy$

29) $\frac{3xz}{y^3} - 6$

30) $14uvt - 14v^2t$

31) $u^4 - 8u^4v + 20u^4w$

32) $\frac{x^2z}{3} + \frac{2x^2}{3} - \frac{2}{3z}$

33) $24m + 2m^2$

34) $e^{2x} - 3xze^{2x} - 4ye^{2x}$

35) $\frac{6x^2}{z} + 4x^2 - \frac{2x^2y}{z}$

36) $x^4 + 2x^3 - x^2$

37) $2v - 6uv + 10v^2w - 2v^2w$

38) $(6x + 8z - 4zxy)$

39) $8x^2 - 4x$

40) 6

Multiplying Binomials

1) $x^2 - x - 20$

2) $x^2 - 9x + 18$

3) $x^2 + 11x + 28$

4) $x^2 - 4x - 21$

5) $6x^2 + 14x - 40$

6) $55x^2 - 2x - 21$

7) $36x^2 - 65x - 36$

8) $x^2 - 4$

9) $x^2 - 4x + 4$

10) $x^2 - x - 20$

11) $3x^2 + 2x - 21$

12) $4x^2 - 11x - 45$

13) $24x^2 + 53x - 7$

14) $x^2 + 3x - 4$

15) $10x^2 - 103x - 77$

16) $-4x^3 + 12x^2 - x + 3$

17) $x^2 + 6x + 9$

18) $x^2 - x$

19) $x^2 + 9x + 18$

20) $2x^2 + 3x - 14$

Factoring Trinomials

1) $(x+3)(x+5)$

2) $(x-2)(x-3)$

3) $(x+4)(x+2)$

4) $(x-2)(x-4)$

5) $(x-4)(x-4)$

6) $(x-3)(x-4)$

7) $(x+2)(x+9)$

8) $(x+6)(x-4)$

9) $(x-2)(x+6)$

10) $(x-1)(x-9)$

11) $(x-2)(x+7)$

12) $(x-9)(x+3)$

13) $(x+3)(x-14)$

14) $(x+11)(x+11)$

15) $(2x+3)(3x-4)$

16) $(x-15)(x-2)$

17) $(3x-1)(x+4)$

18) $(5x-1)(2x+7)$

19) $(x+12)(x+12)$

20) $(4x-1)(2x+3)$

21) $3, 11$

22) $w=2, l=8$

23) $s=2$

Chapter 10:

Exponents and Radicals

Topics that you'll learn in this part:

✓ Multiplication Property of Exponents

✓ Division Property of Exponents

✓ Powers of Products and Quotients

✓ Zero and Negative Exponents

✓ Negative Exponents and Negative Bases

✓ Writing Scientific Notation

✓ Square Roots

Multiplication Property of Exponents

✍ *Simplify*

1) $4x^4 \times 4x^4 \times 4x^4 =$

2) $2x^2 \times x^2 =$

3) $x^4 \times 3x =$

4) $x \times 2x^2 =$

5) $5x^4 \times 5x^4 =$

6) $2yx^2 \times 2x =$

7) $3x^4 \times y^2x^4 =$

8) $y^2x^3 \times y^5x^2 =$

9) $4yx^3 \times 2x^2y^3 =$

10) $6x^2 \times 6x^3y^4 =$

11) $3x^4y^5 \times 7x^2y^3 =$

12) $7x^2y^5 \times 9xy^3 =$

13) $7xy^4 \times 4x^3y^3 =$

14) $3x^5y^3 \times 8x^2y^3 =$

15) $3x \times y^5x^3 \times y^4 =$

16) $yx^2 \times 2y^2x^2 \times 2xy =$

✍ *Solve.*

17) There are 7^6 pieces of leaves on a tree, and there are 7^4 trees in a forest. How many pieces of leaves are there in the forest?

18) In a storage warehouse, each container weights 6^3 pounds. If there are 6^5 containers, how much do the crates weigh in total?

19) You own a microscope with an objective lens and an eyepiece. The objective lens can magnify an object 10^3 times, and the eyepiece can further magnify an object 10^2 times. What is the maximum magnification on your microscope?

20) An asteroid travel at a speed of 8^8 miles per day, how many miles will it travel in 8^3 day?

Division Property of Exponents

✎ *Simplify*

1) $\dfrac{3x^3}{2x^5}$

2) $\dfrac{12x^3}{14x^6}$

3) $\dfrac{12x^3}{9y^8}$

4) $\dfrac{25xy^4}{5x^6y^2}$

5) $\dfrac{2x^4}{7x}$

6) $\dfrac{16x^2y^8}{4x^3}$

7) $\dfrac{12x^4}{15x^7y^9}$

8) $\dfrac{12yx^4}{10yx^8}$

9) $\dfrac{16x^4y}{9x^8y^2}$

✎ *Solve.*

10) Dalloway's room has the dimensions $3a^7$ by, $4b^3$ by, $5b^2$. What is the volume of Dalloway's room?

11) The fuel tank of Mr. Lee's car has the dimensions b^5 by $3c^2$ by $2c^3$. What is the volume of the fuel tank?

12) A factory produces wardrobes and likes to use exponents as dimensions. The wardrobes have the dimensions b^4 by b^4 by $5c^6$. What is the volume of the wardrobes?

13) The annual corn yield is $5a^2kg$ per hectare. If there are $2b^8$ hectares of corn field in Nebraska and $7b^7$ hectares of corn field in Illinois, what is the total annual corn yield in these two states?

14) The dimensions of a water tank are a^2mm by a^5mm by $3b^2$mm. If 1ml water may contain $3c^{21}$ water molecules, how many water molecules are there in the water tank?

Powers of Products and Quotients

✒️ *Simplify.*

1) $(2yx^2)^3 =$

2) $(2z^3y^3x)^4 =$

3) $\left(\frac{x^2yz}{4}\right)^3 =$

4) $(a^{10}b^3c)^2 =$

5) $(2x^2zy^5)^3 =$

6) $\left(\frac{2x}{z^2}y^4\right)^5 =$

7) $(2r^5q^2t^2)^3 =$

8) $\left(\frac{3x^2yz^4}{2m^4n}\right)^3 =$

9) $(10^2 . 10^3)^8 =$

10) $(3^a . 3^b)^4 =$

11) $\left(2x^3y^{10}\frac{z}{3}\right)^3 =$

12) $(xz^4y^{10})^5 =$

13) $\left(\frac{m^6n^4t^3}{2x^2}\right)^5 =$

14) $\left(\frac{i^3j^5k^3}{2ik}\right)^5 =$

15) $(6^5 . 6^2 . 6^0)^2 =$

16) $(e^2 . e^4)^4 =$

17) $\left(t^2\frac{p^2}{q^4}\right)^6 =$

18) $\left(y^5x^4\frac{1}{z^6}\right)^3 =$

19) $\left(\frac{2x.3y}{3z.x^2}\right)^3 =$

20) $(3xy . 4xy)^3 =$

21) $(-j^3 . 2j)^3 =$

22) $(\frac{-2x^2y^2}{z})^3 =$

23) $(-3e^{2t}e^{2\omega t})^3 =$

24) $\left(\frac{25x^{10}y^8}{3z^9}\right)^0 =$

25) $\left(\frac{(-2x)^2}{(-2yz)^3}\right)^3 =$

26) $(4x^2y^4)^4 =$

27) $(2x^4y^4)^3 =$

28) $(3x^2y^2)^2 =$

29) $(3x^4y^3)^4 =$

30) $(2x^6y^8)^2 =$

31) $(12x^3x)^3 =$

32) $(2x^9x^6)^3 =$

33) $(5x^{10}y^3)^3 =$

34) $(4x^3x^3)^2 =$

35) $(3x^3 . 5x)^2 =$

36) $(10x^{11}y^3)^2 =$

37) $(9x^7y^5)^2 =$

38) $(4x^4y^6)^5 =$

39) $(3x . 4y^3)^2 =$

40) $(\frac{5x}{x^2})^2 =$

41) $\left(\frac{x^4y^4}{x^2y^2}\right)^3 =$

42) $\left(\frac{25x}{5x^6}\right)^2 =$

43) $\left(\frac{x^8}{x^6y^2}\right)^2 =$

44) $\left(\frac{xy^2}{x^3y^3}\right)^{-2} =$

45) $\left(\frac{2xy^4}{x^3}\right)^2 =$

46) $\left(\frac{xy^4}{5xy^2}\right)^{-3} =$

47) $((3xyz)^2)^{\frac{1}{2}} =$

48) $(x^2y^2)^{\frac{1}{2}} =$

49) $3x(w^3)^3 =$

50) $\left(\frac{2x}{(2-x)}\right)^2 =$

51) $\left(\frac{2}{3x^2y}\right)^3(y^2x) =$

52) $\frac{(2rq^2)^2}{(-q)^3} =$

53) $\left(\frac{-x^4}{3zy}\right)^2 =$

54) $(2x . x . x^2)^3 =$

55) $(-xy)^2 =$

56) $\frac{(2x^2y)^4}{4x^3} =$

57) $(3x^2)^{t+1} =$

58) $\left(\frac{2tx^2}{3xt^3}\right)^m =$

59) $(3xyz^5)^r =$

Zero and Negative Exponents

✎ Evaluate the following expressions.

1) $8^{-1} =$

2) $8^{-2} =$

3) $2^{-4} =$

4) $10^{-2} =$

5) $9^{-1} =$

6) $3^{-2} =$

7) $7^{-2} =$

8) $3^{-4} =$

9) $6^{-2} =$

10) $5^{-3} =$

11) $22^{-1=}$

12) $4^{-2} =$

13) $5^{-2} =$

14) $35^{-1} =$

15) $4^{-3} =$

16) $6^{-3} =$

17) $3^{-5} =$

18) $5^{-2} =$

19) $2^{-3} =$

20) $3^{-3} =$

21) $7^{-3} =$

22) $6^{-3} =$

23) $8^{-3} =$

24) $9^{-2} =$

25) $10^{-3} =$

26) $10^{-9} =$

27) $(\frac{1}{2})^{-1=}$

28) $(\frac{1}{2})^{-2} =$

29) $(\frac{1}{3})^{-2} =$

30) $(\frac{2}{3})^{-2} =$

31) $(\frac{1}{5})^{-3} =$

32) $(\frac{3}{4})^{-2} =$

33) $(\frac{2}{5})^{-2} =$

34) $(\frac{1}{2})^{-8} =$

35) $(\frac{2}{5})^{-3} =$

36) $(\frac{3}{7})^{-2} =$

37) $(\frac{5}{6})^{-3} =$

38) $\left(\frac{x^2}{e^{-2t}}\right)^{-2} =$

39) $(3xz^{-3})^2 =$

40) $\left(\frac{(a^3)^{-2}}{b}\right)^{-2} =$

41) $\left(\frac{x^2 y}{(-2z)^2}\right)^{-3} =$

42) $\left(\frac{gh^3}{2k}\right)^{-3} =$

43) $\left(\frac{2sqr^2}{2x}\right)^{-1} =$

44) $\left(\frac{25xyz}{33mn^3}\right)^0 =$

45) $(2xy(x^2)^{-2})^{-1} =$

46) $(x^2 z^3)^{-3} =$

47) $\left(\frac{1}{3}xy^2\right)^{-2} =$

48) $\frac{(y^{20}x^{15})^0}{(2x)^{-2}} =$

49) $(-3xy)^{-2} =$

50) $(e^{-\omega t})(e^{\omega t}) =$

51) $(3x + y)^{-2} =$

52) $\frac{(4x+1)^{-1}}{(9x)^{-3}} =$

53) $\left(\frac{2y}{zx}\right)^{-3} =$

54) $\left(\frac{1}{2}\right)^{-5} =$

55) $\left(\frac{3}{(2-2x^2)}\right)^{-2} =$

56) $(\frac{1}{2x+1})^{-1}(2x + 1)^{-1} =$

57) $(1 - x)^{-2} =$

58) $(x^2)^{-2} =$

59) $(x^{-2}zy)^{-2} =$

60) $(x^{-1}z)^2 =$

61) $(yz^{-2})^{-1} =$

62) $(2x)^{-3}(x^2) =$

Writing Scientific Notation

✎ *Write each number in scientific notation.*

1) $0.113 =$

2) $0.02 =$

3) $2.5 =$

4) $20 =$

5) $60 =$

6) $0.004 =$

7) $78 =$

8) $1,600 =$

9) $1,450 =$

10) $91,000 =$

11) $2,000,000 =$

12) $0.0000006 =$

13) $354,000 =$

14) $0.000325 =$

15) $0.00023 =$

16) $56,000,000 =$

17) $21,000 =$

18) $78,000,000 =$

19) $0.0000022 =$

20) $0.00012 =$

21) $0.02 =$

✎ *Solve.*

22) A color photograph taken with a digital camera is converted into digital format using 4×10^0 bytes per pixel. Photographs taken with the camera each have 2.2×10^6 pixels. How many bytes are there in one photo? Write your answer in scientific notation.

23) A certain animated movie earned 1.1×10^9 in revenues at the box office. The movie lasts $\$9.1 \times 10^1$ minute. How much revenue was earned per minute of the movie? Write your final answer in scientific notation

24) The weight of a honeybee is $1.2 \times 10^{-1} g$,. The weight of the pollen collected by the bee on one trip is $6.2 \times 10^{-2} g$. What is the combined weight of the bee and the pollen? Express your answer in scientific notation.

Square Roots

✎ *Find the value each square root.*

1) $\sqrt{1} =$

2) $\sqrt{4} =$

3) $\sqrt{9} =$

4) $\sqrt{25} =$

5) $\sqrt{16} =$

6) $\sqrt{49} =$

7) $\sqrt{36} =$

8) $\sqrt{0} =$

9) $\sqrt{64} =$

10) $\sqrt{81} =$

11) $\sqrt{121} =$

12) $\sqrt{225} =$

13) $\sqrt{144} =$

14) $\sqrt{100} =$

15) $\sqrt{256} =$

16) $\sqrt{289} =$

17) $\sqrt{324} =$

18) $\sqrt{400} =$

19) $\sqrt{900} =$

20) $\sqrt{529} =$

21) $\sqrt{90} =$

✎ *Evaluate.*

22) $8\sqrt{2} \times 2\sqrt{2} =$

23) $6\sqrt{3} - \sqrt{12} =$

24) $3\sqrt{3} + \sqrt{27} =$

25) $\sqrt{8} - \sqrt{2} =$

26) $\sqrt{27} \times \sqrt{3} =$

27) $4\sqrt{5} + \sqrt{25} =$

28) $\sqrt{169} - \sqrt{13} =$

29) $\sqrt{81} - \sqrt{3} =$

30) $\sqrt{144} + \sqrt{12} =$

31) $\sqrt{289} - \sqrt{17} =$

32) $3\sqrt{18} - 3\sqrt{2} =$

33) $\frac{3\sqrt{3}}{\sqrt{3}} =$

34) $\frac{\sqrt{4} \times \sqrt{2}}{3\sqrt{2}} =$

35) $\sqrt{36} - 5\sqrt{6} =$

36) $\sqrt{121} - 2\sqrt{11} =$

37) $\sqrt{10} \times \sqrt{6} =$

38) $\sqrt{3} \times \sqrt{5} =$

39) $\sqrt{11} \times \sqrt{3} =$

40) $\sqrt{7} + \sqrt{28} =$

✎ *Solve.*

41) Which of the following is equal to the square root of 75?

A. $2\sqrt{6}$

B. $36\sqrt{2}$

C. $5\sqrt{3}$

D. $12\sqrt{6}$

Answers of Worksheets

Multiplication Property of Exponents

1) $64x^{12}$
2) $2x^4$
3) $3x^5$
4) $2x^3$
5) $25x^8$

6) $4x^3y$
7) $3x^8y^2$
8) x^5y^7
9) $8x^5y^4$
10) $36x^5y^4$

11) $21x^6y^8$
12) $63x^3y^8$
13) $28x^4y^7$
14) $24x^7y^6$
15) $3x^4y^9$

16) $4x^5y^4$
17) 7^{10}
18) 6^8
19) 10^5
20) 8^{11}

Division Property of Exponents

1) $\frac{3}{2x^2}$
2) $\frac{6}{7x^3}$
3) $\frac{4x^3}{3y^8}$
4) $\frac{5y^2}{x^5}$

5) $\frac{2x^3}{7}$
6) $\frac{4y^8}{x}$
7) $\frac{4}{5x^3y^9}$
8) $\frac{6}{5x^4}$

9) $\frac{16}{9x^4y}$
10) $60a^7b^5$
11) $6b^5c^5$
12) $5b^8c^6$
13) $10a^2b^8 +$

$35a^2b^7$
14) $9a^7b^2c^{21}$
15) $4b^6c^3$

Powers of Products and Quotients

1) $8y^3x^6$
2) $16z^{12}y^{12}x^4$
3) $\frac{x^6y^3z^3}{64}$
4) $a^{20}b^6c^2$
5) $8x^6z^3y^{15}$
6) $\frac{32x^5}{z^{10}}y^{20}$
7) $8r^{15}q^6t^6$
8) $\frac{27x^6y^3z^{12}}{8m^{12}n^3}$
9) 10^{40}
10) $3^{4(a+b)}$
11) $8x^9y^{30}\frac{z^3}{27}$

12) $x^5z^{20}y^{50}$
13) $\frac{m^{30}n^{20}t^{15}}{32x^{10}}$
14) $\frac{i^{10}j^{15}k^{10}}{32}$
15) 6^{14}
16) e^{24}
17) $t^{12}\frac{p^{12}}{q^{24}}$
18) $y^{15}x^{12}\frac{1}{z^{18}}$
19) $\frac{8y^3}{z^3.x^3}$
20) $1728x^6y^6$
21) $-8j^{12}$
22) $\frac{-8x^6y^6}{z^3}$

23) $-27e^{6t(1+\omega)}$
24) 1
25) $\frac{x^6}{-8y^9z^9}$
26) $256x^8y^{16}$
27) $8x^{12}y^{12}$
28) $9x^4y^4$
29) $81x^{16}y^{12}$
30) $4x^{12}y^{16}$
31) $1,728x^{12}$
32) $8x^{45}$
33) $125x^{30}y^9$
34) $16x^{12}$

35) $225x^8$
36) $100x^{22}y^6$
37) $81x^{14}y^{10}$
38) $1,024x^{20}y^{30}$
39) $144x^2y^6$
40) $\frac{25}{x^2}$
41) x^6y^6
42) $\frac{25}{x^{10}}$
43) $\frac{x^4}{y^4}$
44) x^4y^2
45) $\frac{4y^8}{x^4}$

46) $\frac{125}{y^6}$

47) $3xyz$

48) xy

49) $3xw^6$

50) $\frac{4x^2}{(2-x)^2}$

51) $\frac{8}{27x^5y}$

52) $-2r^2q$

53) $\frac{x^8}{9z^2y^2}$

54) $8x^{12}$

55) x^2y^2

56) $4x^5y^4$

57) $3^{t+1}x^{2t+2}$

58) $\frac{2^m x^m}{3^m t^{2m}}$

59) $3^r x^r y^r z^{5r}$

Zero and Negative Exponents

1) $\frac{1}{8}$

2) $\frac{1}{64}$

3) $\frac{1}{16}$

4) $\frac{1}{100}$

5) $\frac{1}{9}$

6) $\frac{1}{9}$

7) $\frac{1}{49}$

8) $\frac{1}{81}$

9) $\frac{1}{36}$

10) $\frac{1}{125}$

11) $\frac{1}{22}$

12) $\frac{1}{16}$

13) $\frac{1}{25}$

14) $\frac{1}{35}$

15) $\frac{1}{64}$

16) $\frac{1}{216}$

17) $\frac{1}{243}$

18) $\frac{1}{25}$

19) $\frac{1}{8}$

20) $\frac{1}{27}$

21) $\frac{1}{343}$

22) $\frac{1}{216}$

23) $\frac{1}{512}$

24) $\frac{1}{81}$

25) $\frac{1}{1,000}$

26) $\frac{1}{1,000,000,000}$

27) 2

28) 4

29) 9

30) $\frac{9}{4}$

31) 125

32) $\frac{16}{9}$

33) $\frac{25}{4}$

34) 256

35) $\frac{125}{8}$

36) $\frac{49}{9}$

37) $\frac{216}{125}$

38) $\frac{1}{e^{4t}x^2}$

39) $\frac{9x^2}{z^6}$

40) $a^{12}b^2$

41) $\frac{64z^6}{x^6y^3}$

42) $\frac{8k^3}{g^3h^9}$

43) $\frac{x}{sqr^2}$

44) 1

45) $\frac{x^3}{2y}$

46) $\frac{1}{x^6z^9}$

47) $\frac{9}{x^2y^4}$

48) $4x^2$

49) $\frac{1}{9x^2y^2}$

50) 1

51) $\frac{1}{(3x+y)^2}$

52) $\frac{729x^3}{4x+1}$

53) $\frac{z^3x^3}{8y^3}$

54) 32

55) $\frac{(2-2x^2)^2}{9}$

56) 1

57) $\frac{1}{(1-x)^2}$

58) $\frac{1}{x^4}$

59) $\frac{x^4}{z^2y^2}$

60) $\frac{z^2}{x^2}$

61) $\frac{z^2}{y}$

62) $\frac{1}{8x}$

Writing Scientific Notation

1) 1.13×10^{-1}

2) 2×10^{-2}

3) 2.5×10^0

4) 2×10^1

5) 6×10^1

6) 4×10^{-3}

7) 7.8×10^1

8) 1.6×10^3

9) 1.45×10^3

10) 9.1×10^4

11) 2×10^6

12) 6×10^{-7}

13) 3.54×10^5

14) 3.25×10^{-4}

15) 2.3×10^{-4}

16) 5.6×10^7

17) 2.1×10^4

18) 7.8×10^7

19) 2.2×10^{-6}

20) 1.2×10^{-4}

21) 2×10^{-2}

22) 8.8×10^6

23) 1.21×10^7

24) 1.8×10^{-1}

Square Roots

1) 1

2) 2

3) 3

4) 5

5) 4

6) 7

7) 6

8) 0

9) 8

10) 9

11) 11

12) 15

13) 12

14) 10

15) 16

16) 17

17) 18

18) 20

19) 30

20) 23

21) $3\sqrt{10}$

22) 32

23) $4\sqrt{3}$

24) $6\sqrt{3}$

25) $\sqrt{2}$

26) 9

27) $4\sqrt{5} + 5$

28) $13 - \sqrt{13}$

29) $9 - \sqrt{3}$

30) $12 + 2\sqrt{3}$

31) $17 - \sqrt{17}$

32) $6\sqrt{2}$

33) 3

34) $\frac{2}{3}$

Section 3:

Geometry and Statistics

- *Plane Figures*

- *Solid Figures*

- *Statistics*

- *Probability*

Chapter 11:

Plane Figures

Topics that you'll learn in this part:

- ✓ Transformations: Translations, Rotations, and Reflections
- ✓ The Pythagorean Theorem
- ✓ Area of Triangles
- ✓ Perimeter of Polygons
- ✓ Area and Circumference of Circles
- ✓ Area of Squares, Rectangles, and Parallelograms
- ✓ Area of Trapezoids

Transformations: Translations, Rotations, and Reflections

✍️ *Graph the image of the figure using the transformation given.*

1) translation: 4 units right

   and 1 unit down

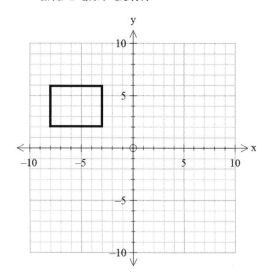

2) translation: 4 units left

   and 2 unit up

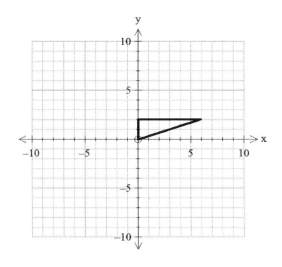

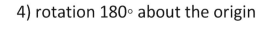

3) rotation 90∘ counterclockwise about the origin

4) rotation 180∘ about the origin

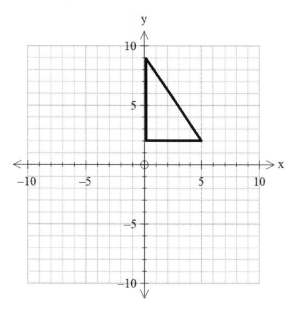

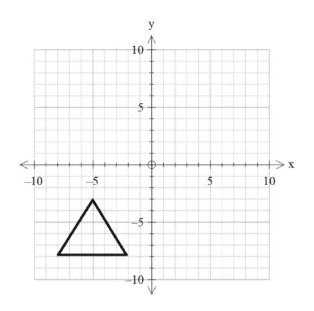

The Pythagorean Theorem

✍️ *Do the following lengths form a right triangle?*

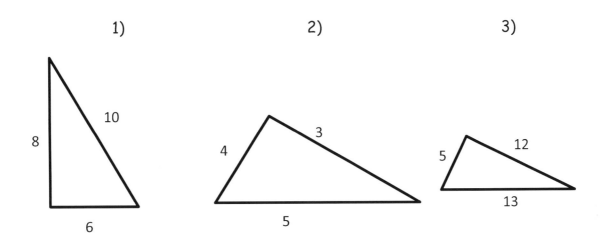

1)

8

10

6

2)

4

3

5

3)

5

12

13

✍️ *Find each missing length to the nearest tenth.*

4)

8

?

15

5)

?

34

16

6)

12

9

?

Area of Triangles

📝 *Find the area of each.*

1)

$c = 12\ mi$
$h = 4\ mi$

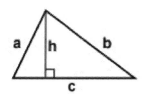

2)

$s = 15\ m$
$h = 9m$

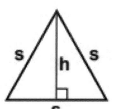

3)

$a = 5\ m$
$b = 11\ m$
$c = 14\ m$
$h = \ \ 4\ m$

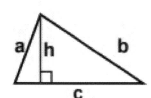

4)

$s = 10\ m$
$h = 8.6\ m$

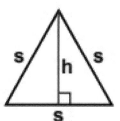

5)

$c = 15\ mi$
$h = 6\ mi$

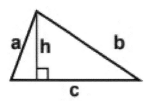

6)

$a = 5\ m$
$h = 4\ m$
$b = 9$
$C = 12$

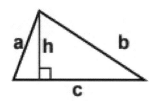

7)

$c = 8\ mi$
$h = 4\ mi$

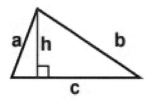

8)

$s = 10\ m$
$h = 8\ m$

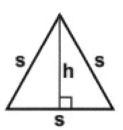

Perimeter of Polygon

✏️ *Find the perimeter of each shape.*

1)

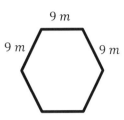

9 m
9 m   9 m

2)

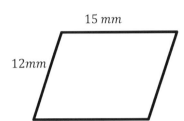

15 mm
12mm

3)

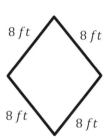

8 ft   8 ft
8 ft   8 ft

4)

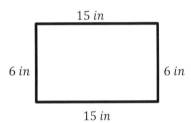

15 in
6 in   6 in
15 in

5)

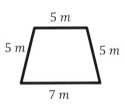

5 m
5 m   5 m
7 m

6)

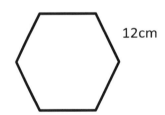

12cm

7)

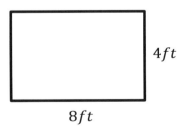

4ft
8ft

8)

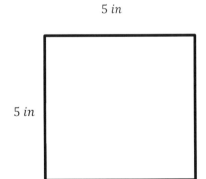

5 in
5 in

Area and Circumference of Circles

✎ *Find the area and circumference of each.* (π = 3.14)

1)

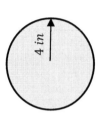

2)

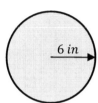

3)

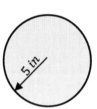

4)

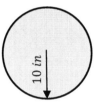

✎ *Find the area and of each.* (π = 3.14)

5)

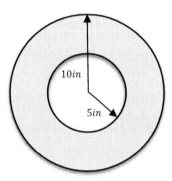

6)

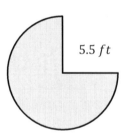

7)

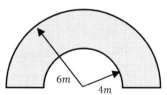

8)

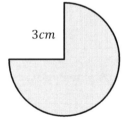

Area of Squares, Rectangles, and Parallelograms

✎ *Find the area of each.*

1)

12 yd

21yd   21yd

12yd

2)

17mi

17 mi   17 mi

17 mi

3)

12.3 ft

13.5ft

6 ft

13.5 ft

12.3 ft

4)

3.8 in

6.3 in

5)

14m

8m   10

6)

6m

3m

Area of Trapezoids

🖎 *Calculate the area for each trapezoid.*

1)

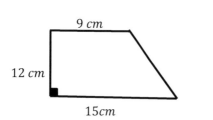

9 cm

12 cm

15cm

2)

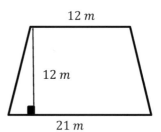

12 m

12 m

21 m

3)

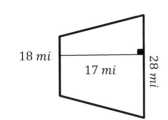

18 mi

17 mi

28 mi

4)

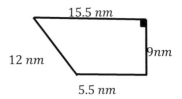

15.5 nm

12 nm

9nm

5.5 nm

5)

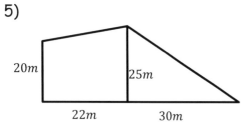

20m

25m

22m   30m

6)

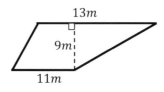

13m

9m

11m

7)

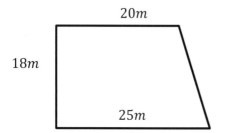

20m

18m

25m

8)

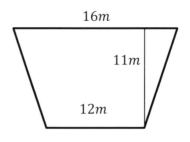

16m

11m

12m

Answers of Worksheets

Transformations

1) translation:

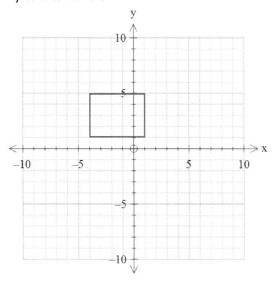

2) translation:

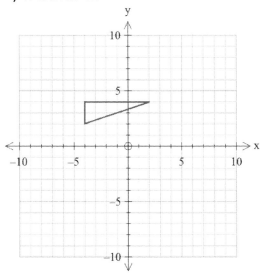

3) rotation 90∘ counterclockwise about the origin

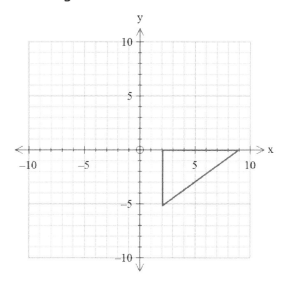

4) rotation 180∘ about the origin

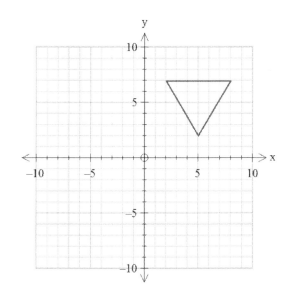

The Pythagorean Theorem

1) yes

2) yes

3) yes

4) 17

5) 30

6) 15

Area of Triangles

1) $24mi^2$
2) $67.5\,m2$
3) $28\,m2$
4) $43\,m2$
5) $45m^2$
6) $24m^2$
7) $16mi^2$
8) $40m^2$

Perimeter of Polygons

1) $54\,m$
2) $54\,mm$
3) $32\,ft$
4) $42\,in$
5) $22m$
6) $72cm$
7) $24ft$
8) $20in$

Area and Circumference of Circles

1) $Area: 50.26\,in^2, Circumference: 25.12\,in$
2) $Area: 113.1in^2, Circumference: 31.7in$
3) $Area: 78.5in^2, Circumference: 31.4\,in$
4) $Area: 314.16in^2, Circumference: 62.83in$
5) $Area: 235.62in^2$
6) $Area: 71.27\,ft^2$
7) $Area: 31.415m^2$
8) $Area: 21.2cm^2$

Area of Squares, Rectangles, and Parallelograms

1) $252\,yd^2$
2) $289\,mi^2$
3) $81\,ft^2$
4) $23.94\,in^2$
5) $112m^2$
6) $45m^2$

Area of Trapezoids

1) $144cm^2$
2) $198\,m^2$
3) $391\,mi^2$
4) $94.5\,nm^2$
5) $870m^2$
6) $108m^2$
7) $405m^2$
8) $154m^2$

Chapter 12:

Solid Figures

Topics that you'll learn in this part:

- ✓ Volume of Cubes and Rectangle Prisms
- ✓ Surface Area of Cubes
- ✓ Surface Area of a Prism
- ✓ Volume of Pyramids and Cones
- ✓ Surface Area of Pyramids and Cones

Volume of Cubes and Rectangle Prisms

✍ *Find the volume of each of the rectangular prisms.*

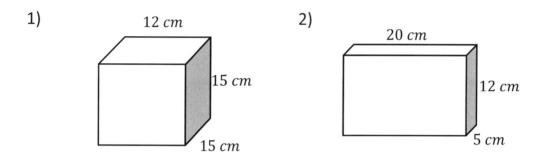

1)   12 cm   2)   20 cm
       15 cm   12 cm
       15 cm   5 cm

✍ *Solve.*

3) Layla wants to build a wooden box with a volume of 45 cubic centimeters. She started with a width of 3cm. How long should Layla make the box?

4) The sea turtle habitat at the zoo is made by connecting two large aquariums. The first aquarium is 6m long, 4m wide, and 2m high. The second aquarium is 8m long, 9m wide, and 3m high. How many cubic meters of space do the sea turtles have in their habitat?

5) The closet is 6 feet wide, 5 feet deep and 8 feet tall. In the closet, there is a suitcase that is 2 feet wide, 3 feet long and 4 feet tall. How much room is left in the closet?

6) Find the volume of the rectangular prism.

Surface Area of Cubes

✎ *Find the surface of each cube.*

1)

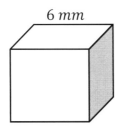

6 mm

2)

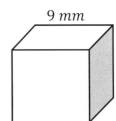

9 mm

3)

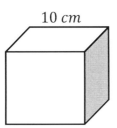

10 cm

4)

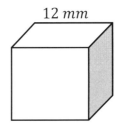

12 mm

5)

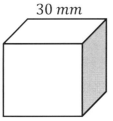

30 mm

6)

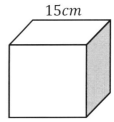

15cm

7)

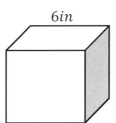

6in

8)

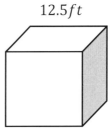

12.5ft

9)

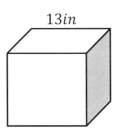

13in

10)

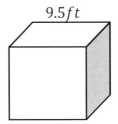

9.5ft

Surface Area of a Prism

📝 *Find the surface of each prism.*

1)

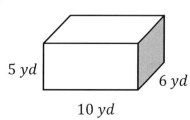

5 yd
6 yd
10 yd

2)

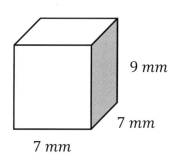

9 mm
7 mm
7 mm

3)

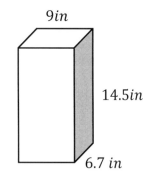

9in
14.5in
6.7 in

4)

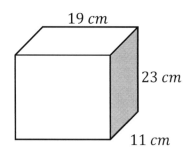

19 cm
23 cm
11 cm

5)

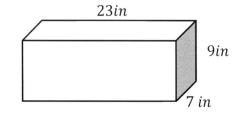

23in
9in
7 in

6)

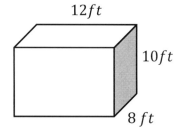

12ft
10ft
8 ft

7)

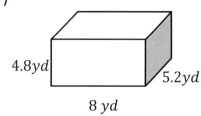

4.8yd
5.2yd
8 yd

8)

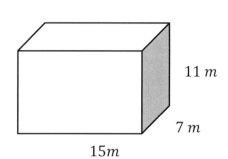

11 m
7 m
15m

Volume of Pyramids and Cones

✍️ *Find the volume of each figure.* (π = 3.14)

1)

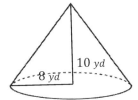

2)

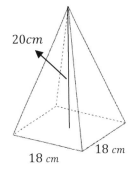

3)

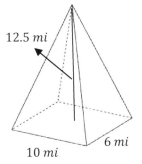

4)

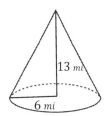

5)

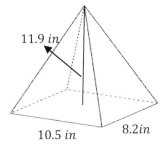

6)

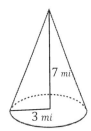

7)

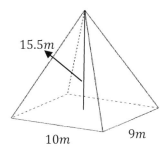

8)

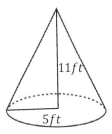

Answers of Worksheets

Volume of Cubes and Rectangle Prisms

1) $2,700cm^3$ 3) 5   5) 216
2) $1,200cm^3$ 4) 264   6) 140

Surface Area of a Cube

1) $216\,mm^2$ 5) $5,400\,mm^2$ 9) $1,014\,in^2$
2) $486\,mm^2$ 6) $1,350\,cm^2$ 10) $541.5\,ft^2$
3) $600\,cm^2$ 7) $216\,in^2$
4) $864\,mm^2$ 8) $937.5\,ft^2$

Surface Area of a Prism

1) $240\,yd^2$ 3) $576.6\,in^2$ 5) $736\,in^2$ 7) $209.92\,yd^2$
2) $350\,mm^2$ 4) $1,798\,cm^2$ 6) $592\,ft^2$ 8) $694\,m^2$

Volume of Pyramids and Cones

1) $670.2\,yd^3$ 3) $250mi^3$ 5) $341.5in^3$ 7) $465m^3$
2) $2,160cm^3$ 4) $490.1mi^3$ 6) $65.97mi^3$ 8) $288ft^3$

Chapter 13:

Statistics

Topics that you'll learn in this part:

✓ Mean, Median, Mode, and Range of the Given Data

✓ First Quartile, Second Quartile and Third Quartile of the Given Data

✓ Bar Graph

✓ Box and Whisker Plots

✓ Stem–And–Leaf Plot

✓ The Pie Graph or Circle Graph

✓ Scatter Plots

Mean, Median, Mode, and Range of the Given Data

✍ **Find Mean, Median, Mode, and Range of the Given Data.**

1) 7, 2, 5, 1, 1, 2, 3, 4

2) 2, 2, 2, 3, 6, 3, 7, 4

3) 9, 4, 3, 1, 7, 9, 4, 6, 4

4) 8, 4, 2, 4, 3, 2, 4, 5

5) 8, 5, 7, 5, 7, 9, 8, 8, 6

6) 5, 1, 4, 4, 9, 2, 9, 1, 2, 5, 1, 8

7) 4, 7, 5, 9, 5, 7, 7, 7, 5, 2, 3, 5

8) 7, 5, 4, 9, 6, 7, 7, 5, 2, 8

9) 2, 5, 5, 6, 2, 4, 7, 6, 4, 9, 5

10) 10, 5, 2, 5, 4, 5, 8, 10, 8

11) 4, 5, 2, 2, 6, 8, 10, 12

12) 5, 9, 5, 9, 8, 6, 11, 9, 6, 8

13) 14, 16, 16, 15, 19, 16

14) 10, 9, 12, 13, 13, 17, 15, 10

15) 3, 2, 9, 8, 5, 5, 6, 8

16) 14, 16, 18, 17, 12, 16, 15, 16

17) 9, 18, 17, 15, 14, 19, 18, 17

18) 15, 12, 18, 17, 15, 15, 12, 14

19) 32, 51, 38, 69, 15, 50, 38, 8

20) 1, 9, 8, 6, 5, 9, 8, 9

✍ **Solve.**

21) A stationery sold 14 pencils, 40 red pens, 50 blue pens, 10 notebooks, 16 erasers, 38 rulers and 36 color pencils. What are the Mode and Range for the stationery sells?

22) In an English test, eight students score 14, 13, 17, 11, 19, 20, 14 and 15. What are their Median, Mode and Range?

23) Bob has 12 black pen, 14 red pen, 15 green pens, 24 blue pens and 3 boxes of yellow pens. If the Mean and Median are 16 and 15 respectively, what is the number of yellow pens in each box?

Box and Whisker Plot

✎ *Make box and whisker plots for the given data.*

1) 11,17,22,18,23,2,3,16,21,7,8,15,5

2) 33,31,30,38,40,36

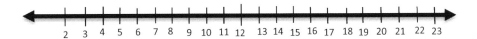

3) 46,36,15,21,65,25,48,70,68

4) 9,10,12,15,17,19,24,26,28

5) 41,43,45,47,51,50,44

6) 60,66,62,65,68,70,72

7) 72,82,81,76,77,82,84,79,80

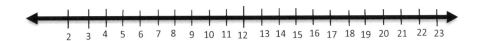

Bar Graph

> 📝 *Graph the given information as a bar graph.*

1) The number of bed-sheets manufactured by a factory during five consecutive weeks is given below. Draw the bar graph representing the above data.

week	First	Second	Third	Fourth	Fifth
Number of bed-sheets	550	810	680	320	850

2) The number of students in 7 different classes is given below. Represent this data on the bar graph.

class	6th	7th	8th	9th	10th	11th	12th
Number of students	125	115	130	140	145	100	80

3) The number of trees planted by Eco-club of a school in different years is given below. Draw the bar graph to represent the data.

Year	2005	2006	2007	2008	2009	2010
Number of trees to be planted	150	220	350	400	300	380

4) The following data represents the sale of refrigerator sets in a showroom in first 6 months of the year. Draw the bar graph for the data given and find out the months in which the sale was minimum and maximum.

Months	Jan	Feb	March	April	May	June
No. of refrigerator sold	19	21	12	46	35	28

Stem–And–Leaf Plot

✎ *Make stem ad leaf plots for the given data.*

1) 74,88,97,72,79,86,95,79,83,91

Stem	Leaf plot

2) 37,48,26,33,49,26,19,26,48

Stem	Leaf plot

3) A zookeeper created the following stem-and-leaf plot showing the number of tigers at each major zoo in the country. What was the smallest number of tigers at any one zoo?

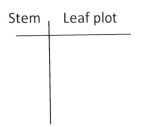

Stem	Leaf plot
0	7
1	1 4 8
2	5 5 5 6 7 7 9
3	
4	

4) The government published the following stem-and-leaf plot showing the number of bears at each major zoo in the country. How many zoos have more than 50 bears?

Stem	Leaf plot
0	
1	8 8
2	1 3 6 6 7 7 9
3	1 7
4	1 4 5 7
5	0 3

The Pie Graph or Circle Graph

✎*Solve.*

1) Suppose you take a poll of the students in your class to find out their favorite foods, and get the following results:

Pizza:41%, Ice Cream:24%, Raw Mushrooms:9%, Dog Food:11%, Chicken Livers:15%

Organize this data in a circle graph.

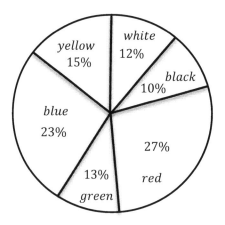

Favorite colors

2) Which color is the most?

3) What percentage of pie graph is yellow?

4) Which color is the least?

5) What percentage of pie graph is blue?

6) What percentage of pie graph is green?

Scatter Plots

🖎 Construct a scatter plot.

1) Construct a graph of the length of the humerus bone vs. the length of the radius.

Length of Radius (cm)	25	22	23.5	22.5	23	22.6	21.4	21.9	23.5	24.3	24
Length of Humerus (cm)	29.7	26.5	27.1	26	28	25.2	24	23.8	26.7	29	27

2) Plot the data on the scatter plot below, choosing appropriate scales and labels.

Age	25	30	35	37	38	40	41	45	55	60	62	65	70	75
Earnings ($)	22000	26500	29500	29000	30000	32000	35000	36000	41000	41000	42500	43000	37000	37500

3) The table shows the numbers of students remaining on an after-school bus and the numbers of minutes since leaving the school.

Minutes	0	5	9	15	23	26	32
Number of students	56	45	39	24	17	6	0

Plot the data from the table on the graph. Describe the relationship between the two data sets.

Answers of Worksheets

Mean, Median, Mode, and Range of the Given Data

1) mean: 3.125, median: 2.5, mode: 1, 2, range: 6

2) mean: 3.625, median: 3, mode: 2, range: 5

3) mean: 5.22, median: 4, mode: 4, range: 8

4) mean: 4, median: 4, mode: 4, range: 6

5) mean: 7, median: 7, mode: 5, 7, 8, range: 4

6) mean: 4.25, median: 4, mode: 1, range: 8

7) mean: 5.5, median: 5, mode: 7.5, range: 7

8) mean: 6, median: 6.5, mode: 7, range: 7

9) mean: 5, median: 5, mode: 5, range: 7

10) mean: 6.33, median: 5, mode: 5, range: 8

11) mean: 6.125, median: 2, mode: 2, range: 10

12) mean: 7.6, median:8, mode: 9, range: 6

13) mean: 16, median:16, mode: 16, range: 5

14) mean: 12.375, median:12.5, mode: 10,13, range: 8

15) mean: 5.75, median:5.5, mode:8,5, range: 7

16) mean: 15.5, median:16, mode: 16, range: 6

17) mean: 15.875, median:17, mode: 18,17, range: 10

18) mean: 14.75, median:15, mode: 15, range: 6

19) mean: 37.625, median:38, mode: 38, range: 61

20) mean: 6.875, median:8, mode: 9, range: 8

21) Mode: none, range:40

22) median:14.5, mode:14, range:9

23) 5

Box and Whisker Plots

1)

2)

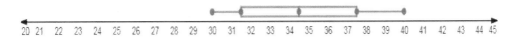

3)

4)

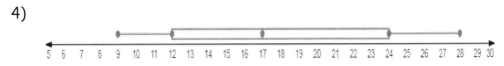

5)

6)

7)

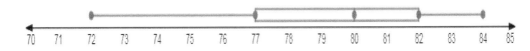

Bar Graph

1)

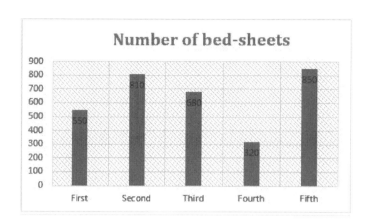

2)

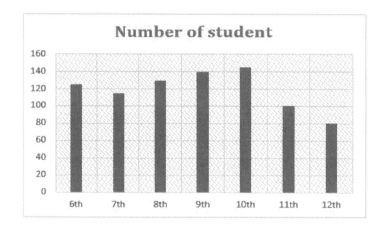

3)

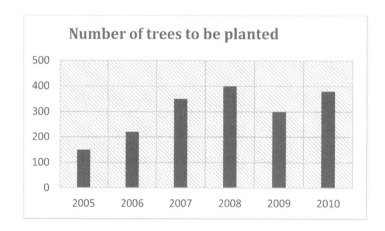

4)

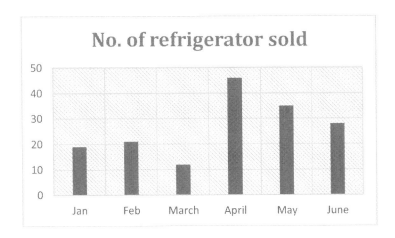

Stem–And–Leaf Plot

1)

Stem	leaf
7	2 4 9 9
8	3 6 8
9	1 5 7

2)

Stem	leaf
1	9
2	6 6 6
3	3 7
4	8 8 9

3)

Stem	leaf
4	1 2
5	3 4 4 8
6	5 5 7 9

4) 7
5) 1

The Pie Graph or Circle Graph

1)

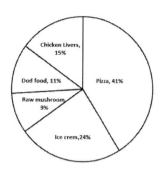

2) red

3) 15%

4) black

5) 23%

6) 13%

Scatter Plots

1)

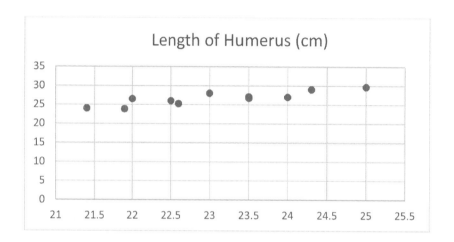

2)

3)

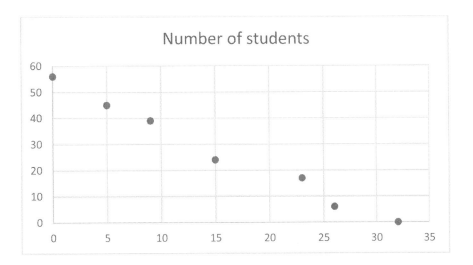

When time increase, number of students decrease

Chapter 14:

Probability

Topics that you'll learn in this part:

✓ Probability of Simple Events

✓ Experimental Probability

✓ Independent and Dependent Events Word Problems

✓ Factorials

✓ Permutations

✓ Combination

Probability of Simple Events

![Solve icon] *Solve.*

1) A number is chosen at random from 1 to 50. Find the probability of selecting multiples of 10.

2) You spin the spinner shown below once. Each sector shown has an equal area. What is P (shaded sector)?

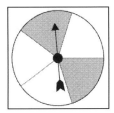

3) You draw a card at random from a deck that contains 3 black cards and 7 red cards. What is the probability of choosing a black card?

4) Greg has an MP3 player called the Jumble. The Jumble randomly selects a song for the user to listen to. Greg's Jumble has 6 classical songs, 7 rock songs, and 9 rap songs on it. What is P (not a rap song)?

5) Omar ordered his sister a birthday card from a company that randomly selects a card from their inventory. The company has 21 total cards in inventory.14 of those cards are birthday cards. What is P (not a birthday card)?

6) Giovanna owns a farm. She is going to randomly select one animal to present at the state fair. She has 6 pigs, 7 chickens, and 10 cows. What is What is the probability of choosing a chicken?

Experimental Probability

🖎 *Solve.*

1) A bag contains 18 balls: two green, five black, eight blue, a brown, a red and one white. If 17 balls are removed from the bag at random, what is the probability that a brown ball has been removed?

A. $\frac{1}{9}$ C. $\frac{16}{17}$

B. $\frac{1}{6}$ D. $\frac{17}{18}$

2) The table shows the number of feathers Patsy the Peacock sold at each of the 8 festivals this year. Based on this data, what is a reasonable estimate of the probability that Patsy sells fewer than 5 feathers next festival?

3	6	1	4
2	3	7	2

3) The Cinemania theater showed 108 different movies last year. Of those, 15 movies were action movies. Based on this data, what is a reasonable estimate of the probability that the next movie is an action movie?

4) Stephen read 12 books, 20 magazines, and 17 newspaper articles last year. Based on this data, what is a reasonable estimate of the probability that Stephen's next reading material is a magazine?

5) March Madness Movies served 23 lemonades out of a total of 111 fountain drinks last weekend. Based on this data, what is a reasonable estimate of the probability that the next fountain drink ordered is a lemonade?

Factorials

✎ *Determine the value for each expression*

1) $\frac{9!}{6!}$

2) $\frac{10!}{8!}$

3) $\frac{7!}{3!}$

4) $\frac{5!}{4!}$

5) $\frac{6!+2!}{4!}$

6) $3! \times 4!$

✎ *Solve.*

7) While playing Scrabble®, you need to make a word out of the letters A N P S. How many arrangements of these letters are possible?

8) How many ways can you have your quarter pound hamburger prepared if you can have it prepared with or without mustard, ketchup, mayonnaise, lettuce, tomatoes, pickles, cheese, and onions?

9) How many arrangements of all the letters in the word PYRAMID do not end with D?

10) Five students are running for Junior Class President. They must give speeches before the election committee. In how many different orders could they give their speeches?

11) How many five-letter "words" can be formed from the letters in the word COMBINE?

12) In how many ways can six different algebra books and three different geometry books be arranged on a shelf if all the books of one subject must remain together?

Combinations and Permutations

✎ Calculate.

1) 4! = ____

2) 4! × 3! = ____

3) 5! = ____

4) 6! + 3! = ____

5) 7! = ____

6) 8! = ____

7) 4! + 4! = ____

8) 4! − 3! = ____

✎ Solve.

9) Susan is baking cookies. She uses sugar, flour, butter, and eggs. How many different orders of ingredients can she try? _____

10) Jason is planning for his vacation. He wants to go to museum, watch a movie, go to the beach, and play volleyball. How many different ways of ordering are there for him? _____

11) How many 5-digit numbers can be named using the digits 1, 2, 3, 4, and 5 without repetition? _____

12) In how many ways can 5 boys be arranged in a straight line? _____

13) In how many ways can 4 athletes be arranged in a straight line? _____

14) A professor is going to arrange her 7 students in a straight line. In how many ways can she do this? _____

15) How many code symbols can be formed with the letters for the word WHITE? _____

16) In how many ways a team of 8 basketball players can to choose a captain and co-captain? _____

Answers of Worksheets

Probability of simple events

1) $\frac{5}{10}$ 2) $\frac{2}{5}$ 3) $\frac{3}{10}$ 4) $\frac{13}{22}$ 5) $\frac{7}{21}$ 6) $\frac{1}{23}$

Experimental Probability

1) $\frac{17}{18}$ 2) 0.75   3) $\frac{15}{108}$ 4) $\frac{20}{49}$ 5) $\frac{23}{111}$

Factorials

1) 504	4) 5	7) 24	10) 120
2) 90	5) 30.08	8) 256	11) 2520
3) 840	6) 144	9) 4320	12) 720

Combination and Permutations

1) 24	7) 48	13) 24
2) 144	8) 18	14) 5,040
3) 120	9) 24	15) 120
4) 726	10) 24	16) 56
5) 5,040	11) 120	
6) 40,320	12) 120	

AFOQT Test Review

The Air Force Officer Qualifying Test (AFOQT) is a standardized test to assess skills and personality traits that have proven to be predictive of success in officer commissioning programs such as the training program.

The AFOQT is used to select applicants for officer commissioning programs, such as Officer Training School (OTS) or Air Force Reserve Officer Training Corps (Air Force ROTC) and pilot and navigator training.

The AFOQT is a multiple-aptitude battery that measures developed abilities and helps predict future academic and occupational success in the military. The AFOQT is a multiple-choice test which consists of 12 subtests and two of them are Arithmetic Reasoning and Mathematics Knowledge.

In this section, there are 2 complete Arithmetic Reasoning and Mathematics Knowledge AFOQT Tests. Take these tests to see what score you'll be able to receive on a real AFOQT test.

Good luck!

AFOQT Math Practice Tests

Time to Test

Time to refine your quantitative reasoning skill with a practice test

In this section, there are two complete AFOQT Mathematics practice tests. Take these tests to simulate the test day experience. After you've finished, score your tests using the answer keys.

Before You Start

- You'll need a pencil and a timer to take the test.

- For each question, there are four possible answers. Choose which one is best.

- It's okay to guess. There is no penalty for wrong answers.

- Use the answer sheet provided to record your answers.

- After you've finished the test, review the answer key to see where you went wrong.

Calculators are NOT permitted for the AFOQT Test

Good Luck!

AFOQT Math Practice Test 1 Answer Sheet

Remove (or photocopy) this answer sheet and use it to complete the practice test.

AFOQT Mathematics Practice Test 1 Answer Sheet

AFOQT Practice Test 1 — Arithmetic Reasoning

1	Ⓐ Ⓑ Ⓒ Ⓓ Ⓔ	11	Ⓐ Ⓑ Ⓒ Ⓓ Ⓔ	21	Ⓐ Ⓑ Ⓒ Ⓓ Ⓔ
2	Ⓐ Ⓑ Ⓒ Ⓓ Ⓔ	12	Ⓐ Ⓑ Ⓒ Ⓓ Ⓔ	22	Ⓐ Ⓑ Ⓒ Ⓓ Ⓔ
3	Ⓐ Ⓑ Ⓒ Ⓓ Ⓔ	13	Ⓐ Ⓑ Ⓒ Ⓓ Ⓔ	23	Ⓐ Ⓑ Ⓒ Ⓓ Ⓔ
4	Ⓐ Ⓑ Ⓒ Ⓓ Ⓔ	14	Ⓐ Ⓑ Ⓒ Ⓓ Ⓔ	24	Ⓐ Ⓑ Ⓒ Ⓓ Ⓔ
5	Ⓐ Ⓑ Ⓒ Ⓓ Ⓔ	15	Ⓐ Ⓑ Ⓒ Ⓓ Ⓔ	25	Ⓐ Ⓑ Ⓒ Ⓓ Ⓔ
6	Ⓐ Ⓑ Ⓒ Ⓓ Ⓔ	16	Ⓐ Ⓑ Ⓒ Ⓓ Ⓔ		
7	Ⓐ Ⓑ Ⓒ Ⓓ Ⓔ	17	Ⓐ Ⓑ Ⓒ Ⓓ Ⓔ		
8	Ⓐ Ⓑ Ⓒ Ⓓ Ⓔ	18	Ⓐ Ⓑ Ⓒ Ⓓ Ⓔ		
9	Ⓐ Ⓑ Ⓒ Ⓓ Ⓔ	19	Ⓐ Ⓑ Ⓒ Ⓓ Ⓔ		
10	Ⓐ Ⓑ Ⓒ Ⓓ Ⓔ	20	Ⓐ Ⓑ Ⓒ Ⓓ Ⓔ		

AFOQT Practice Test 1 — Mathematics Knowledge

1	Ⓐ Ⓑ Ⓒ Ⓓ Ⓔ	11	Ⓐ Ⓑ Ⓒ Ⓓ Ⓔ	21	Ⓐ Ⓑ Ⓒ Ⓓ Ⓔ
2	Ⓐ Ⓑ Ⓒ Ⓓ Ⓔ	12	Ⓐ Ⓑ Ⓒ Ⓓ Ⓔ	22	Ⓐ Ⓑ Ⓒ Ⓓ Ⓔ
3	Ⓐ Ⓑ Ⓒ Ⓓ Ⓔ	13	Ⓐ Ⓑ Ⓒ Ⓓ Ⓔ	23	Ⓐ Ⓑ Ⓒ Ⓓ Ⓔ
4	Ⓐ Ⓑ Ⓒ Ⓓ Ⓔ	14	Ⓐ Ⓑ Ⓒ Ⓓ Ⓔ	24	Ⓐ Ⓑ Ⓒ Ⓓ Ⓔ
5	Ⓐ Ⓑ Ⓒ Ⓓ Ⓔ	15	Ⓐ Ⓑ Ⓒ Ⓓ Ⓔ	25	Ⓐ Ⓑ Ⓒ Ⓓ Ⓔ
6	Ⓐ Ⓑ Ⓒ Ⓓ Ⓔ	16	Ⓐ Ⓑ Ⓒ Ⓓ Ⓔ		
7	Ⓐ Ⓑ Ⓒ Ⓓ Ⓔ	17	Ⓐ Ⓑ Ⓒ Ⓓ Ⓔ		
8	Ⓐ Ⓑ Ⓒ Ⓓ Ⓔ	18	Ⓐ Ⓑ Ⓒ Ⓓ Ⓔ		
9	Ⓐ Ⓑ Ⓒ Ⓓ Ⓔ	19	Ⓐ Ⓑ Ⓒ Ⓓ Ⓔ		
10	Ⓐ Ⓑ Ⓒ Ⓓ Ⓔ	20	Ⓐ Ⓑ Ⓒ Ⓓ Ⓔ		

AFOQT Mathematics Practice Test 2 Answer Sheet

AFOQT Practice Test 2 Arithmetic Reasoning

1	Ⓐ Ⓑ Ⓒ Ⓓ Ⓔ	11	Ⓐ Ⓑ Ⓒ Ⓓ Ⓔ	21 Ⓐ Ⓑ Ⓒ Ⓓ Ⓔ
2	Ⓐ Ⓑ Ⓒ Ⓓ Ⓔ	12	Ⓐ Ⓑ Ⓒ Ⓓ Ⓔ	22 Ⓐ Ⓑ Ⓒ Ⓓ Ⓔ
3	Ⓐ Ⓑ Ⓒ Ⓓ Ⓔ	13	Ⓐ Ⓑ Ⓒ Ⓓ Ⓔ	23 Ⓐ Ⓑ Ⓒ Ⓓ Ⓔ
4	Ⓐ Ⓑ Ⓒ Ⓓ Ⓔ	14	Ⓐ Ⓑ Ⓒ Ⓓ Ⓔ	24 Ⓐ Ⓑ Ⓒ Ⓓ Ⓔ
5	Ⓐ Ⓑ Ⓒ Ⓓ Ⓔ	15	Ⓐ Ⓑ Ⓒ Ⓓ Ⓔ	25 Ⓐ Ⓑ Ⓒ Ⓓ Ⓔ
6	Ⓐ Ⓑ Ⓒ Ⓓ Ⓔ	16	Ⓐ Ⓑ Ⓒ Ⓓ Ⓔ	
7	Ⓐ Ⓑ Ⓒ Ⓓ Ⓔ	17	Ⓐ Ⓑ Ⓒ Ⓓ Ⓔ	
8	Ⓐ Ⓑ Ⓒ Ⓓ Ⓔ	18	Ⓐ Ⓑ Ⓒ Ⓓ Ⓔ	
9	Ⓐ Ⓑ Ⓒ Ⓓ Ⓔ	19	Ⓐ Ⓑ Ⓒ Ⓓ Ⓔ	
10	Ⓐ Ⓑ Ⓒ Ⓓ Ⓔ	20	Ⓐ Ⓑ Ⓒ Ⓓ Ⓔ	

AFOQT Practice Test 2 Mathematics Knowledge

1	Ⓐ Ⓑ Ⓒ Ⓓ Ⓔ	11	Ⓐ Ⓑ Ⓒ Ⓓ Ⓔ	21 Ⓐ Ⓑ Ⓒ Ⓓ Ⓔ
2	Ⓐ Ⓑ Ⓒ Ⓓ Ⓔ	12	Ⓐ Ⓑ Ⓒ Ⓓ Ⓔ	22 Ⓐ Ⓑ Ⓒ Ⓓ Ⓔ
3	Ⓐ Ⓑ Ⓒ Ⓓ Ⓔ	13	Ⓐ Ⓑ Ⓒ Ⓓ Ⓔ	23 Ⓐ Ⓑ Ⓒ Ⓓ Ⓔ
4	Ⓐ Ⓑ Ⓒ Ⓓ Ⓔ	14	Ⓐ Ⓑ Ⓒ Ⓓ Ⓔ	24 Ⓐ Ⓑ Ⓒ Ⓓ Ⓔ
5	Ⓐ Ⓑ Ⓒ Ⓓ Ⓔ	15	Ⓐ Ⓑ Ⓒ Ⓓ Ⓔ	25 Ⓐ Ⓑ Ⓒ Ⓓ Ⓔ
6	Ⓐ Ⓑ Ⓒ Ⓓ Ⓔ	16	Ⓐ Ⓑ Ⓒ Ⓓ Ⓔ	
7	Ⓐ Ⓑ Ⓒ Ⓓ Ⓔ	17	Ⓐ Ⓑ Ⓒ Ⓓ Ⓔ	
8	Ⓐ Ⓑ Ⓒ Ⓓ Ⓔ	18	Ⓐ Ⓑ Ⓒ Ⓓ Ⓔ	
9	Ⓐ Ⓑ Ⓒ Ⓓ Ⓔ	19	Ⓐ Ⓑ Ⓒ Ⓓ Ⓔ	
10	Ⓐ Ⓑ Ⓒ Ⓓ Ⓔ	20	Ⓐ Ⓑ Ⓒ Ⓓ Ⓔ	

AFOQT Math Test 1

Arithmetic Reasoning

- ○ **25 questions**

- ○ **Total time for this section:** 29 Minutes

- ○ **Calculators are not allowed at the test.**

1) A writer finishes 198 pages of his manuscript in 18 hours. How many pages is his average per hour?

   A. 9   C. 11

   B. 10   D. 12

2) If a rectangle is 12 feet by 27 feet, what is its area?

   A. 324   C. 678

   B. 452   D. 750

3) Aria was hired to teach four identical math courses, which entailed being present in the classroom 44 hours altogether. At $36 per class hour, how much did Aria earn for teaching one course?

   A. $144   C. $396

   B. $176   D. $1,584

4) A family owns 8 dozen of magazines. After donating 32 magazines to the public library, how many magazines are still with the family?

   A. 64   C. 118

   B. 96   D. 124

5) Karen is 6 years older than her sister Michelle, and Michelle is 3 years younger than her brother David. If the sum of their ages is 45, how old is Michelle?

   A. 12   C. 29

   B. 23   D. 36

6) John is driving to visit his mother, who lives 450 miles away. How long will the drive be, round–trip, if John drives at an average speed of 60 mph?

   A. 75 Minutes   C. 750 Minutes

   B. 450 Minutes   D. 900 Minutes

7) If one acre of forest contains 124 pine trees, how many pine trees are contained in 19 acres?

    A. 2,356   C. 4,415

    B. 3,207   D. 4,712

8) You are asked to chart the temperature during an 8-hour period to give the average. These are your results:

    7 am: 4 degrees   11 am: 24 degrees

    8 am: 7 degrees   12 pm: 36 degrees

    9 am: 14 degrees   1 pm: 39 degrees

    10 am: 19 degrees   2 pm: 41 degrees

    What is the average temperature?

    A. 23   C. 32

    B. 25   D. 44

9) A woman owns a dog walking business. If 5 workers can walk 15 dogs, how many dogs can 8 workers walk?

    A. 15   C. 24

    B. 18   D. 75

10) Each year, a cyber café charges its customers a base rate of $12, with an additional $0.15 per visit for the first 30 visits, and $0.10 for every visit after that. How much does the cyber café charge a customer for a year in which 45 visits are made?

    A. $12   C. $23

    B. $18   D. $45

11) If a vehicle is driven 45 miles on Monday, 33 miles on Tuesday, and 27 miles on Wednesday, what is the average number of miles driven each day?

    A. 25 Miles   C. 35 Miles

    B. 31 Miles   D. 39 Miles

12) Three co-workers contributed $9.85, $15.45, and $12.75 respectively to purchase a retirement gift for their boss. What is the maximum amount they can spend on a gift?

   A. $38.05

   B. $39.85

   C. $40.25

   D. $42.95

13) While at work, Emma checks her email once every 40 minutes. In 8–hour, how many times does she check her email?

   A. 6 Times

   B. 8 Times

   C. 10 Times

   D. 12 Times

14) Julie gives 6 pieces of candy to each of her friends. If Julie gives all her candy away, which amount of candy could have been the amount she distributed?

   A. 98

   B. 128

   C. 210

   D. 385

15) In the deck of cards, there are 5 spades, 3 hearts, 10 clubs, and 7 diamonds. What is the probability that William will pick out a spade?

   A. $\frac{1}{9}$

   B. $\frac{1}{7}$

   C. $\frac{1}{6}$

   D. $\frac{1}{5}$

16) William is driving a truck that can hold 10 tons maximum. He has a shipment of food weighing 27,000 pounds. How many trips will he need to make to deliver all of the food?

   A. 1 Trip

   B. 3 Trips

   C. 4 Trips

   D. 5 Trips

17) A man goes to a casino with $145. He loses $30 on blackjack, then loses another $40 on roulette. How much money does he have left?

   A. $75

   B. $105

   C. $115

   D. $120

18) Will has been working on a report for 5 hours each day, 7 days a week for 3 weeks. How many minutes has will worked on his report?

A. 4,700 Minutes

C. 6,854 Minutes

B. 6,300 Minutes

D. 7,560 Minutes

19) What is the prime factorization of 378?

A. $2 \times 2 \times 3 \times 7$

C. $2 \times 3 \times 5 \times 5 \times 7$

B. $2 \times 3 \times 3 \times 3 \times 7$

D. $3 \times 3 \times 5 \times 7 \times 7$

20) Camille uses a 25% off coupon when buying a sweater that costs $80. If she also pays 9% sales tax on the purchase, how much does she pay?

A. $20

C. $36.75

B. $24.8

D. $65.4

21) I've got 28 quarts of milk and my family drinks 2 gallons of milk per week. How many weeks will that last us?

A. 2 Weeks

C. 3.5 Weeks

B. 2.25 Weeks

D. 4.5 Weeks

22) A floppy disk shows 987,345 bytes free and 879,621 bytes used. If you delete a file of size 397,756 bytes and create a new file of size 487,236 bytes, how many free bytes will the floppy disk have?

A. 89,480

C. 987,345

B. 745,874

D. 1,076,825

23) Ten out of 50 students had to go to summer school. What is the ratio of students who did not have to go to summer school expressed, in its lowest terms?

A. $\frac{1}{5}$

C. $\frac{4}{5}$

B. $\frac{1}{4}$

D. $\frac{5}{4}$

24) If a circle has a diameter of 2 feet, what is its circumference?

A. 2π C. 8π

B. 4π D. 12π

25) Ava needs $\frac{1}{4}$ of an ounce of salt to make 1 cup of dip for fries. How many cups of dip will she be able to make if she has 60 ounces of salt?

A. 15   C. 85

B. 60   D. 240

IF YOU FINISH BEFORE TIME IS CALLED, YOU MAY CHECK YOUR WORK ON THIS SECTION ONLY. DO NOT TURN TO OTHER SECTION IN THE TEST. **STOP**

AFOQT Math Practice Test 1

Mathematics Knowledge

○ **25 questions**

○ **Total time for this section:** 22 Minutes

○ **Calculators are not allowed at the test.**

1) In the following diagram what is the value of x?

A. 30◦

B. 45◦

C. 60◦

D. 90◦

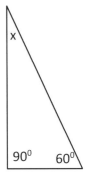

2) What is the value of $\sqrt{81} \times \sqrt{49}$?

A. 6   C. 63

B. $\sqrt{130}$ D. $\sqrt{87}$

3) If a = 5, what is the value of b in this equation?

$$b = \frac{a^3}{5} - 2$$

A. 5   C. 15

B. 13   D. 23

4) Which of the following is an obtuse angle?

A. 35◦   C. 145◦

B. 105◦   D. 175◦

5) Which of the following is not equal to 3^2?

A. 3 squared   C. 3 to the second power

B. the square of 3   D. 3 cubed

6) The fourth root of 625 is:

A. 4   C. 6

B. 5   D. 8

7) A circle has a radius of 4 inches. What is its approximate area? (π = 3.14)

A. 31.41 square inches

C. 78.87 square inches

B. 50.26 square inches

D. 121.2 square inches

8) The volume of this box is:

A. 12 cm³

B. 24 cm³

C. 48 cm³

D. 96 cm³

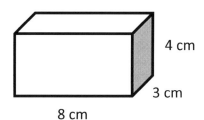

4 cm

3 cm

8 cm

9) If $- 9a = 81$, then $a =$ ___

A. –9

C. 0

B. –8

D. 9

10) A square has one side with length 8 feet. The area of the square is:

A. 16 square feet

C. 64 square feet

B. 32 square feet

D. 128 square feet

11) In the following right triangle, what is the value of x rounded to the nearest hundredth?

A. 2.34

B. 6.70

C. 8.75

D. 9.85

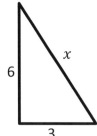

6

x

3

12) $(-3x + 7)(3x - 4)$ = ?

A. $-6x + 3$

C. $-9x^2 - 28$

B. $-9x^2 + 33x - 28$

D. $3x + 5$

13) $3(a - 7) = 34$, what is the value of a?

    A. 3.5   C. 8.75

    B. 7   D. 15

14) If $2^{18} = 2^5 \times 2^x$, what is the value of x?

    A. 2   C. 13

    B. 8   D. 16

15) Factor this expression: $x^2 + 4x - 21$

    A. $x^2(4 - 21)$ C. $(x + 7)(x - 3)$

    B. $x(x + 4 - 21)$ D. $(x - 7)(x + 3)$

16) Find the slope of the line running through the points (4, 4) and (7, 1).

    A. $\frac{1}{3}$ C. 1

    B. -1   D. $-\frac{1}{3}$

17) The cube root of 4,197 is?

    A. 7   C. 70

    B. 17   D. 170

18) What is 87,456 in scientific notation?

    A. 8.7456   C. 8.7456×10^4

    B. 0.087456×10^5 D. 87.456×10^4

19) What's the area of the non-shaded part in the following figure?

    A. 15

    B. 20

    C. 25

    D. 35

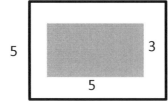

20) A medium pizza has a diameter of 7 inches. What is its circumference?

   A. 3.5π

   B. 7 π

                                C. 14π

                                D. 49π

21) A writer finishes 270 pages of his manuscript in 45 hours. How many pages is his average per hour?

   A. 6

   B. 8

                                C. 9

                                D. 12

22) Which of the following sets of factors do both 56 and 18 have in common?

   A. {1, 2}

   B. {6, 9, 14}

                                C. {0, 1, 2, 3}

                                D. {1, 3, 4, 18}

23) What is the circumference of a circle with center at point A if the distance from point X to Y is 10 feet? (π = 3.14)

   A. 3.14 Feet

   B. 15.7 Feet

   C. 31.4 Feet

   D. 314 Feet

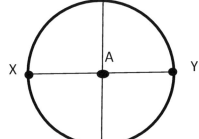

24) In the following diagram, the straight line is divided by one angled line at 45∘. What is the value of a.

   A. 45∘

   B. 90∘

   C. 135∘

   D. 150∘

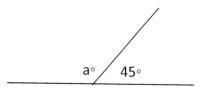

25) What's the square root of $49x^4$?

A. $7\sqrt{x}$

C. $7x^2$

B. $7x$

D. $7x^4$

IF YOU FINISH BEFORE TIME IS CALLED, YOU MAY CHECK YOUR WORK ON THIS SECTION ONLY. DO NOT TURN TO OTHER SECTION IN THE TEST. **STOP**

AFOQT Math Test 2

Arithmetic Reasoning

○ **25 questions**

○ **Total time for this section:** 29 Minutes

○ **Calculators are not allowed at the test.**

1) In a classroom of 50 students, 38 are female. What percentage of the class is male?

   A. 12%   C. 30%

   B. 24%   D. 38%

2) How many square feet of tile is needed for a 12 feet x 14 feet room?

   A. 26 square feet   C. 168 square feet

   B. 144 square feet   D. 356 square feet

3) Will has been working on a report for 5 hours each day, 7 days a week for 2 weeks. How many minutes has Will worked on his report?

   A. 14   C. 4,200

   B. 35   D. 6,300

4) Find the average of the following numbers: 11, 25, 16, 9, 19

   A. 16   C. 80

   B. 19   D. 400

5) Convert 0.038 to a percent.

   A. 0.038%   C. 3.80%

   B. 0.38%   D. 38%

6) James is driving to visit his mother, who lives 280 miles away. How long will the drive be, round–trip, if James drives at an average speed of 56 mph?

   A. 5 minutes   C. 600 minutes

   B. 300 minutes   D. 680 minutes

7) What is the distance in miles of a trip that takes 1.5 hours at an average speed of 55 miles per hour? (Round your answer to a whole number)

   A. 45 miles   C. 82.5 miles

   B. 55 miles   D. 110 miles

8) You are asked to chart the temperature during a 6-hour period to give the average. These are your results:

7 am: 3 degrees

8 am: 5 degrees

9 am: 11 degrees

10 am: 16 degrees

11 am: 23 degrees

12 pm: 29 degrees

What is the average temperature?

A. 10.5

B. 14.5

C. 21.5

D. 24.75

9) The hour hand of a watch rotates 30 degrees every hour. How many complete rotations does the hour hand make in 6 days?

A. 12

B. 14

C. 18

D. 24

10) During the last week of track training, Emma achieves the following times in seconds: 58, 67, 49, 69, 53, and 57. Her three best times this week (least times) are averaged for her final score on the course. What is her final score?

A. 49 seconds

B. 53 seconds

C. 57 seconds

D. 58 seconds

11) With what number must 1.78456 be multiplied in order to obtain the number 178.456?

A. 100

B. 1,000

C. 10,000

D. 100,000

12) Which of the following is NOT a factor of 63?

A. 3

B. 5

C. 7

D. 21

13) Emma is working in a hospital supply room and makes $50.00 an hour. The union negotiates a new contract giving each employee a 3% cost of living raise. What is Emma's new hourly rate?

    A. $1.5 an hour

    B. $15 an hour

    C. $51.5 an hour

    D. $53 an hour

14) Emily and Lucas have taken the same number of photos on their school trip. Emily has taken 3 times as many photos as Mia. Lucas has taken 14 more photos than Mia. How many photos has Mia taken?

    A. 3

    B. 7

    C. 14

    D. 42

15) A mobile classroom is a rectangular block that is 45 feet by 25 feet in length and width respectively. If a student walks around the block once, how many yards does the student cover?

    A. 140 yards

    B. 240 yards

    C. 562 yards

    D. 1,125 yards

16) The sum of 5 numbers is greater than 90 and less than 150. Which of the following could be the average (arithmetic mean) of the numbers?

    A. 15

    B. 25

    C. 35

    D. 40

17) What is the product of the square root of 25 and the square root of 64?

    A. 39

    B. 40

    C. 48

    D. 1,600

18) A barista averages making 20 coffees per hour. At this rate, how many hours will it take until she's made 2,200 coffees?

    A. 100 hours

    B. 110 hours

    C. 200 hours

    D. 220 hours

19) There are 90 rooms that need to be painted and only 8 painters available. If there are still 10 rooms unpainted by the end of the day, what is the average number of rooms that each painter has painted?

A. 9

C. 11

B. 10

D. 16

20) Nicole was making $14.5 per hour and got a raise to $15.75 per hour. What percentage increase was Nicole's raise?

A. 1.25%

C. 4.75%

B. 2.5%

D. 8.62%

21) An architect's floor plan uses $\frac{1}{3}$ inch to represent one mile. What is the actual distance represented by $6\frac{1}{2}$ inches?

A. 3.5 miles

C. 17.5 miles

B. 6.5 miles

D. 19.5 miles

22) Will has been working on a report for 6 hours each day, 6 days a week for 3 weeks. How many minutes has Will worked on his report?

A. 2,160 minutes

C. 6,480 minutes

B. 3,240 minutes

D. 6,820 minutes

23) A snack machine accepts only quarters. Candy bars cost 35¢, a package of peanuts costs 65¢, and a can of cola costs 25¢. How many quarters are needed to buy two Candy bars, one package of peanuts, and one can of cola?

A. 5 quarters

C. 7 quarters

B. 6 quarters

D. 9 quarters

24) If $-3y + 2y + 5y = -18$, then what is the value of y?

A. −7.5

C. −4.5

B. −5.4

D. 0

25) A bread recipe calls for $3\frac{2}{5}$ cups of flour. If you only have $1\frac{1}{2}$ cups of flour, how much more flour is needed?

A. $\frac{1}{3}$

C. 1

B. $\frac{1}{2}$

D. 1.9

IF YOU FINISH BEFORE TIME IS CALLED, YOU MAY CHECK YOUR WORK ON THIS SECTION ONLY. DO NOT TURN TO ANY OTHER SECTION IN THE TEST. **STOP**

AFOQT Math Practice Test 2

Mathematics Knowledge

- ○ **25 questions**
- ○ **Total time for this section:** 22 Minutes
- ○ **Calculators are not allowed at the test.**

1) The cube root of 729 is?

    A. 9

    B. 81

    C. 729

    D. 6,561

2) $(x - 4)(x + 3) = ?$

    A. $x^2 + 7x + 12$

    B. $2x + 7x + 12$

    C. $x^2 + x - 1$

    D. $x^2 - x - 12$

3) A circle has a diameter of 14 inches. What is its approximate area? ($\pi = 3.14$)

    A. 21.98

    B. 43.96

    C. 153.86

    D. 615.44

4) Convert 36,000 to scientific notation.

    A. 3.60×10^{-4}

    B. 36×10^4

    C. 3.6×10^4

    D. 36×10^5

5) What is the perimeter of the triangle in the provided diagram?

    A. 65

    B. 105

    C. 1,000

    D. 2,000

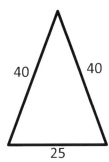

6) A rectangular plot of land is measured to be 120 feet by 180 feet. Its total area is:

    A. 300 square feet

    B. 3,200 square feet

    C. 21,600 square feet

    D. 32,000 square feet

7) If x is a positive integer divisible by 5, and $x < 50$, what is the greatest possible value of x?

    A. 25

    B. 35

    C. 40

    D. 45

8) There are two pizza ovens in a restaurant. Oven 1 burns three times as many pizzas as oven 2. If the restaurant had a total of 12 burnt pizzas on Saturday, how many pizzas did oven 2 burn?

   A. 3   C. 12

   B. 4   D. 36

9) Which of the following is an obtuse angle?

   A. $45°$ C. $195°$

   B. $98°$ D. $270°$

10) $3^5 \times 3^4 = ?$

   A. 3^1 C. 3^{12}

   B. 3^9 D. 3^{20}

11) What is the sum of the prime numbers in the following list of numbers?

     11, 7, 14, 20, 12, 17, 15, 23, 45

   A. 18   C. 35

   B. 23   D. 58

12) One fourth the cube of 5 is:

   A. 25   C. 50.75

   B. 31.25   D. 125

13) What is 324.2735 rounded to the nearest tenth?

   A. 324   C. 324.273

   B. 324.27   D. 324.3

14) Which of the following is the correct calculation for 5!?

   A. $5 \times 4 \times 3 \times 2 \times 1$ C. $5 \times 4 \times 3 \times 2 \times 1 \times 0$

   B. $1 \times 2 \times 3 \times 4$ D. $0 \times 1 \times 2 \times 3 \times 4 \times 5$

15) Convert 50% to a fraction.

    A. $\frac{1}{4}$

    B. $\frac{1}{2}$

    C. $\frac{2}{3}$

    D. $\frac{3}{4}$

16) The equation of a line is given as: $y = -3x + 2$. Which of the following points does not lie on the line?

    A. (-1, 5)

    B. (−2, 8)

    C. (2, 5)

    D. (3, -7)

17) How long is the line segment shown on the number line below?

    A. −9

    B. −3

    C. 3

    D. 9

-10 -9 -8 -7 -6 -5 -4 -3 -2 -1 0 1 2 3 4 5 6 7 8 9 10

18) Simplify: $3(2x^7)^3$.

A. $5x^{10}$

B. $6x^{10}$

C. $8x^{21}$

D. $24x^{21}$

19) What is the distance between the points (3, 1) and (−5, 7)?

    A. 8

    B. 10

    C. 14

    D. 24

20) $x^2 - 64 = 0$, x could be:

    A. −6

    B. −8

    C. 12

    D. 16

21) With what number must 11.73245 be multiplied in order to obtain the number 11,732.45?

    A. 10

    B. 100

    C. 1,000

    D. 10,000

22) Which of the following is NOT a factor of 30?

    A. 3   C. 15

    B. 5   D. 16

23) The sum of 3 numbers is greater than 160 and less than 190. Which of the following could be the average (arithmetic mean) of the numbers?

    A. 30   C. 55

    B. 45   D. 70

24) The supplement angle of a $35°$ angle is:

    A. $70°$ C. $145°$

    B. $105°$ D. $180°$

25) 25% of 24 is:

    A. 6   C. 12

    B. 8   D. 20

IF YOU FINISH BEFORE TIME IS CALLED, YOU MAY CHECK YOUR WORK ON THIS SECTION ONLY. DO NOT TURN TO ANY OTHER SECTION IN THE TEST. **STOP**

FAOQT Mathematics Practice Tests

Answers and Explanations

AFOQT Math Practice Test 1 - AFOQT							
Arithmetic Reasoning				Mathematics Knowledge			
1)	C	16)	B	1)	A	16)	B
2)	A	17)	A	2)	C	17)	B
3)	C	18)	B	3)	D	18)	C
4)	A	19)	B	4)	B	19)	B
5)	A	20)	D	5)	D	20)	B
6)	D	21)	C	6)	B	21)	A
7)	A	22)	D	7)	B	22)	A
8)	A	23)	C	8)	D	23)	C
9)	C	24)	B	9)	A	24)	C
10)	B	25)	D	10)	C	25)	C
11)	C			11)	B		
12)	A			12)	B		
13)	D			13)	D		
14)	C			14)	C		
15)	D			15)	C		

AFOQT Math Practice Test 2 - AFOQT

Arithmetic Reasoning				Mathematics Knowledge			
1)	B	16)	B	1)	C	16)	C
2)	C	17)	B	2)	D	17)	D
3)	C	18)	B	3)	C	18)	D
4)	A	19)	B	4)	C	19)	B
5)	C	20)	D	5)	B	20)	B
6)	C	21)	D	6)	C	21)	C
7)	C	22)	C	7)	D	22)	D
8)	B	23)	A	8)	C	23)	C
9)	A	24)	C	9)	B	24)	C
10)	B	25)	D	10)	B	25)	A
11)	A			11)	D		
12)	B			12)	B		
13)	C			13)	D		
14)	B			14)	A		
15)	A			15)	B		

AFOQT Math Practice Tests Explanations

In this section, answers and explanations are provided for the AFOQT Practice Math Tests. Review the answers and explanations to learn more about solving AFOQT Math questions fast.

AFOQT Math Practice Test 1 Arithmetic Reasoning

Answers and Explanations

1) Choice C is correct

$\frac{198}{18} = 11$

2) Choice A is correct

Area of a rectangle = width × length = 12 × 27 = 324

3) Choice C is correct

44 ÷ 4 = 11 hours for one course, 11 × 36 = 396 ⟹ $396

4) Choice A is correct

8 dozen of magazines are 96 magazines: 8 × 12 = 96, 96 − 32 = 64

5) Choice A is correct

Michelle = Karen − 6, Michelle = David − 3, Karen + Michelle + David = 45

Karen = Michelle + 6, David = Michelle + 3, Karen + Michelle + David = 45

Now, replace the ages of Karen and David by Michelle. Then:

Michelle + 6 + Michelle + Michelle + 3 = 45, 3Michelle + 9 = 45 ⟹ 3Michelle = 45 − 9

3Michelle = 36, Michelle = 12

6) Choice D is correct

$$distance = speed \times time \Rightarrow \text{time} = \frac{distance}{speed} = \frac{900}{60} = 15$$

(Round trip means that the distance is 900 miles)

The round trip takes 15 hours. Change hours to minutes, then: $15 \times 60 = 900$

7) Choice A is correct

Write proportion and solve. $\frac{1}{124} = \frac{19}{x} \Rightarrow x = 19 \times 124 = 2{,}356$

8) Choice A is correct

$average = \frac{sum}{total}$, Sum = 4 + 7 + 14 + 19 + 24 + 36 + 39 + 41 = 184

Total number of numbers = 8, $average = \frac{184}{8} = 23$

9) Choice C is correct

Each worker can walk 3 dogs: 15 ÷ 5 = 3, 8 workers can walk 24 dogs. 8 × 3 = 24

10) Choice B is correct

The base rate is $12. The fee for the first 30 visits is: $30 \times 0.15 = 4.5$

The fee for the visits 31 to 45 is: $15 \times 0.10 = 1.5$, Total charge: 12 + 4.5 + 1.5 = 18

11) Choice C is correct

$$average = \frac{sum}{total} = \frac{45 + 33 + 27}{3} = \frac{105}{3} = 35$$

12) Choice A is correct

The amount they have = $9.85 + $15.45 + $12.75 = 38.05

13) Choice D is correct

Change 8 hours to minutes, then: 8 × 60 = 480 minutes, $\frac{480}{40} = 12$

14) Choice C is correct

Since Julie gives 6 pieces of candy to each of her friends, then, then number of pieces of candies must be divisible by 6.

A. 98 ÷ 6 = 16.33
B. 128 ÷ 6 = 21.33
C. 210 ÷ 6 = 35
D. 385 ÷ 6 = 64.166

Only choice C gives a whole number.

15) Choice D is correct

$$probability = \frac{desired\ outcomes}{possible\ outcomes} = \frac{5}{5 + 3 + 10 + 7} = \frac{5}{25} = \frac{1}{5}$$

16) Choice B is correct

1 ton = 2,000 pounds, 10 ton = 20,000 pounds, $\frac{27,000}{10,000} = 2.7$

William needs to make at least 3 trips to deliver all of the food.

17) Choice A is correct

$145 - 30 - 40 = 75$

18) Choice B is correct

3 weeks = 21 days, $21 \times 5 = 105$ hours, $105 \times 60 = 6,300$ minutes

19) Choice B is correct

Find the value of each choice:

A. $2 \times 2 \times 3 \times 7 = 84$

B. $2 \times 3 \times 3 \times 3 \times 7 = 378$

C. $2 \times 3 \times 5 \times 5 \times 7 = 1,050$

D. $3 \times 3 \times 5 \times 7 \times 7 = 1,960$

20) Choice D is correct

$25\% \times 80 = \frac{25}{100} \times 80 = 20$,

The coupon has $20 value. Then, the selling price of the sweater is $60.

$80 - 20 = 60$, Add 9% tax, then: $\frac{9}{100} \times 60 = 5.4$ for tax, Total: $60 + 5.4 = \$65.4$

21) Choice C is correct

1 quart = 0.25 gallon, 28 quarts = $28 \times 0.25 = 7$ gallons, then: $\frac{7}{2} = 3.5$ weeks

22) Choice D is correct

The difference of the file added, and the file deleted is:

$487,236 - 397,756 = 89,480$, $987,345 + 89,480 = 1,076,825$

23) Choice C is correct

40 students did not have to go to summer school. $50 - 10 = 40$, $\frac{40}{50} = \frac{4}{5}$

24) Choice B is correct

Diameter = $2r \Rightarrow 4 = 2r \Rightarrow r = 2$, Circumference = $2\pi r \Rightarrow C = 2\pi (2) \Rightarrow C = 4\pi$

25) Choice D is correct

Write a proportion and solve. $\frac{\frac{1}{4}}{1} = \frac{60}{x}$ $x = \frac{60}{\frac{1}{4}} = 240$

AFOQT Math Practice Test 1 Mathematics Knowledge

Answers and Explanations

1) Choice A is correct

All angles in a triable add up to 180 degrees. $90° + 60° = 150° \Rightarrow x = 180° - 150° = 30°$

2) Choice C is correct

$\sqrt{81} = 9$, $\sqrt{49} = 7$, $9 \times 7 = 63$

3) Choice D is correct

If a = 5 then: $b = \frac{a^3}{5} - 2 \Rightarrow$ $b = \frac{5^3}{5} - 2 = 25 - 2 = 23$

4) Choice B is correct

An obtuse angle is an angle of greater than 90 degrees and less than 180 degrees. Only choice A is an obtuse angle.

5) Choice D is correct

Only choice D is not equal to 3^2

6) Choice B is correct

$\sqrt[4]{625} = 5$, $(5^4 = 5 \times 5 \times 5 \times 5 = 625)$

7) Choice B is correct

(r = radius) Area of a circle = $\pi r^2 = \pi \times (4)^2 = 3.14 \times 16 = 50.26$

8) Choice D is correct

Volume = length × width × height, Volume = 8 × 3 × 4, Volume = 96 cm³

9) Choice A is correct

$$-9a = 81 \quad \Rightarrow \quad a = \frac{81}{-9} = -9$$

10) Choice C is correct

Area of a square = (one side)² $\Rightarrow$ A = (8)² $\Rightarrow$ A = 64

11) Choice B is correct

Use Pythagorean Theorem: a² + b² = c² $\Rightarrow$ (6)² + (3)² = c² $\Rightarrow$ 36 + 9 = 45 = C² $\Rightarrow$ C = $\sqrt{45}$ = 6.708

12) Choice B is correct

Use FOIL (first, out, in, last) method.

$$(-3x + 7)(3x - 4) = -9x^2 + 12x + 21x - 28 = -9x^2 + 33x - 28$$

13) Choice D is correct

$3(a-7) = 34 \Rightarrow 3a - 21 = 34 \Rightarrow 3a = 34 + 21 = 45 , \Rightarrow 3a = 45 \Rightarrow a = \frac{45}{3} = 15$

14) Choice C is correct

Use exponent multiplication rule: $x^a . x^b = x^{a+b}$

Then: $2^{18} = 2^5 \times 2^x = 2^{5+x} \Rightarrow 18 = 5 + x \Rightarrow x = 18 - 5 = 13$

15) Choice C is correct

To factor the expression $x^2 + 4x - 21$, we need to find two numbers whose sum is 4 and their product is −21. Those numbers are 7 and −3. Then: $x^2 + 4x - 21 = (x + 7)(x - 3)$

16) Choice B is correct

Slope of a line: $\frac{y_2 - y_1}{x_2 - x_1} = \frac{rise}{run}$, $\frac{y_2 - y_1}{x_2 - x_1} = \frac{1 - 4}{7 - 4} = \frac{-3}{3} = -1$

17) Choice B is correct

$\sqrt[3]{4,913}$ = 17

18) Choice C is correct

In scientific notation form, numbers are written with one whole number times 10 to the power of a whole number. Number 87,456 has 5 digits. Write the number and after the first digit put the decimal point. Then, multiply the number by 10 to the power of 4 (number of remaining digits). Then: 87,456 = 8.7456 × 10⁴

19) Choice B is correct

The area of the non-shaded region is equal to the area of the bigger rectangle subtracted by the area of smaller rectangle.

Area of the bigger rectangle = 5 × 7 = 35

Area of the smaller rectangle = 5 × 3 = 15

Area of the non-shaded region = 35 − 15 = 20

20) Choice B is correct

Diameter = 2r ⇒ 7 = 2r ⇒ r = 3.5, Circumference = 2πr ⇒ C = 2π (3.5) ⇒ C = 7π

21) Choice A is correct

$$average = \frac{sum}{total} = \frac{270}{45} = 6$$

22) Choice A is correct

Factor of 56: {1, 2, 4, 7, 8, 14, 28, 56}

Factor of 18: {1, 2, 3, 6, 9, 18}, Then, factors they have in common is {1, 2}

23) Choice C is correct

Diameter = 2r ⇒ 10 = 2r ⇒ r = 5, Circumference = 2πr ⇒ C = 2π (5) ⇒ C = 10 × 3.14 = 31.4

24) Choice C is correct

The straight line is 180 degrees. Then: a = 180° − 45° = 135°

25) Choice C is correct

$$\sqrt{49x^4} = \sqrt{49} \times \sqrt{x^4} = 7 \times x^2 = 7x^2$$

AFOQT Math Practice Test 2 Arithmetic Reasoning

Answers and Explanations

1) Choice B is correct

$50 - 38 = 12$ male students, $\frac{12}{50} = 0.24$, Change 0.24 to percent ⇒ 0.24 × 100 = 24%

2) Choice C is correct

The area of a 12 feet x 14 feet room is 168 square feet. 12 × 14 = 168

3) Choice C is correct

2 weeks = 14 days, Then: 14 × 5 = 70 hours, 70 × 60 = 4,200 minutes

4) Choice A is correct

Sum = 11 + 25 + 16 + 9 + 19 = 80, $average = \frac{80}{5}$ = 16

5) Choice C is correct

To convert a decimal to percent, multiply it by 100 and then add percent sign (%). 0.038 × 100 = 3.80%

6) Choice C is correct

$$distance = speed \times time \Rightarrow \text{time} = \frac{distance}{speed} = \frac{560}{56} = 10$$

(Round trip means that the distance is 560 miles)

The round trip takes 10 hours. Change hours to minutes, then: $10 \times 60 = 600$

7) Choice C is correct

$$Speed = \frac{distance}{time}, 55 = \frac{distance}{1.5} \Rightarrow distance = 55 \times 1.5 = 82.5$$

Rounded to a whole number, the answer is 82.

8) Choice B is correct

$average = \frac{sum}{total}$, Sum = 3 + 5 + 11 + 16 + 23 + 29 = 87, Total number of numbers = 6, $\frac{87}{6} = 14.5$

9) Choice A is correct

Every day the hour hand of a watch makes 2 complete rotation. Thus, it makes 12 complete rotations in 6 days. 2 × 6 = 12

10) Choice B is correct

Emma's three best times are 49, 53, and 57. The average of these numbers is:

$average = \frac{sum}{total}$, Sum = 49 + 53 + 57 = 159, Total number of numbers = 3,

$$average = \frac{159}{3} = 53$$

11) Choice A is correct

1.78456 × 100 = 178.456

12) Choice B is correct

The factors of 63 are: {1, 3, 7, 9, 21, 63}, 5 is not a factor of 63.

13) Choice C is correct

3 percent of 50 is: $50 \times \dfrac{3}{100} = 1.5$, Emma's new rate is $51.5 \Rightarrow 50 + 1.5 = 51.5$

14) Choice B is correct

Emily = Lucas, Emily = 3 Mia $\Rightarrow$ Lucas = 3 Mia, Lucas = Mia + 14

then: Lucas = Mia + 14 $\Rightarrow$ 3 Mia = Mia + 14, Remove 1 Mia from both sides of the equation. Then: 2 Mia = 14 $\Rightarrow$ Mia = 7

15) Choice A is correct

Perimeter of a rectangle = 2 × length + 2 × width = 2 × 45 + 2 × 25 = 90 + 50 = 140

16) Choice B is correct

Let's review the choices provided and find their sum.

a. 15 × 5 = 75
b. 25 × 5 = 125 $\Rightarrow$ is greater than 90 and less than 150
c. 35 × 5 = 175
d. 40 × 5 = 200

Only choice b gives a number that is greater than 120 and less than 180.

17) Choice B is correct

$\sqrt{25} \times \sqrt{64} = 5 \times 8 = 40$

18) Choice B is correct

$\dfrac{1\ hour}{20\ coffees} = \dfrac{x}{2200} \Rightarrow 20 \times x = 1 \times 2{,}200 \Rightarrow 20x = 2{,}200$

$x = 110$, It takes 110 hours until she's made 2,200 coffees.

19) Choice B is correct

$90 - 10 = 80, \dfrac{80}{8} = 10$

20) Choice D is correct

$percent\ of\ change = \dfrac{change}{original\ number}, 15.75 - 14.50 = 1.25$

$$percent\ of\ change = \frac{1.25}{14.5} = 0.0862 \quad \Rightarrow 0.0862 \times 100 = 8.62\%$$

21) Choice D is correct

Write a proportion and solve. $\frac{\frac{1}{3}inches}{6.5} = \frac{1\ mile}{x}$

Use cross multiplication, then: $\frac{1}{3}x = 6.5 \to x = 19.5$

22) Choice C is correct

18 days, 18 × 6 = 108 hours, 108 × 60 = 6,480 minutes

23) Choice A is correct

Two candy bars costs 35¢ and a package of peanuts cost 65¢ and a can of cola costs 25¢. The total cost is: 35 + 65 + 25 = 125⇒ 125 is equal to 5 quarters. 5 × 25 = 125

24) Choice C is correct

$-3y + 2y + 5y = -18 \quad \Rightarrow 4y = -18 \Rightarrow y = -\frac{18}{4} \Rightarrow y = -4.5$

25) Choice D is correct

$3\frac{2}{5} - 1\frac{1}{2} = \frac{17}{5} - \frac{3}{2} = \frac{34}{10} - \frac{15}{10} = \frac{19}{10} = 1.9$

AFOQT Math Practice Test 2 Mathematics Knowledge

Answers and Explanations

1) Choice C is correct

$\sqrt[3]{729} = 8$

2) Choice D is correct

Use FOIL (First, Out, In, Last) method. $(x - 4)(x + 3) = x^2 + 3x - 4x - 12 = x^2 - x - 12$

3) Choice C is correct

Diameter = 14, then: Radius = 7, Area of a circle = $\pi r^2 \Rightarrow A = 3.14(7)^2 = 153.86$

4) Choice C is correct

In scientific notation form, numbers are written with one whole number times 10 to the power of a whole number. Number 36,000 has 5 digits. Write the number and after the first digit put the decimal point. Then, multiply the number by 10 to the power of 4 (number of remaining digits). Then: $36{,}000 = 3.6 \times 10^4$

5) Choice B is correct

Perimeter of a triangle = side 1 + side 2 + side 3 = 40 + 25 + 40 = 105

6) Choice C is correct

Area of a rectangle = width × length = 120 × 180 = 21,600

7) Choice D is correct

From the choices provided, 35, 40 and 45 are divisible by 5. From these numbers, 45 is the biggest.

8) Choice C is correct

Oven 1 = 3 oven 2, If Oven 2 burns 3 then oven 1 burns 9 pizzas. 3 + 9 = 12

9) Choice B is correct

An obtuse angle is an angle of greater than 90° and less than 180°.

10) Choice B is correct

Use exponent multiplication rule: $x^a . x^b = x^{a+b} \Rightarrow$ Then: $3^5 \times 3^4 = 3^9$

11) Choice D is correct

From the list of numbers, 11, 7, 17, and 23 are prime numbers. Their sum is:

11 + 7 + 17 + 23 = 58

12) Choice B is correct

The cube of $5 = 5 \times 5 \times 5 = 125 \Rightarrow \dfrac{1}{4} \times 125 = 31.25$

13) Choice D is correct

324.2735 rounded to the nearest tenth equals 324.3

(Because 324.27 is closer to 324.3 than 324.2)

14) Choice A is correct

$5! = 5 \times 4 \times 3 \times 2 \times 1$

15) Choice B is correct

$$50\% = \frac{50}{100} = \frac{1}{2}$$

16) Choice C is correct

Let's review the choices provided. Put the values of x and y in the equation.

A. $(-1, 5)$ $\Rightarrow x = -1 \Rightarrow y = 5$ This is true!

B. $(-2, 8)$ $\Rightarrow x = -2 \Rightarrow y = 8$ This is true!

C. $(2, 5)$ $\Rightarrow x = 2 \Rightarrow y = -6$ This is not true!

D. $(3, 7)$ $\Rightarrow x = 3 \Rightarrow y = 7$ This is true!

17) Choice D is correct

$3 - (-6) = 3 + 6 = 9$

18) Choice D is correct

$$3(2x^7)^3 \Rightarrow 3 \times 2^3 \times x^{21} = 24x^{21}$$

19) Choice B is correct

Use distance formula: $d = \sqrt{(x_1 - x_2)^2 + (y_1 - y_2)^2} = \sqrt{(3 - (-5))^2 + (1 - 7)^2}$

$\sqrt{64 + 36} = \sqrt{100} = 10$

20) Choice B is correct

$x^2 - 64 = 0$ $\Rightarrow$ $x^2 = 64$ $\Rightarrow x$ could be 8 or -8.

21) Choice C is correct

Number 11.73245 should be multiplied by 1,000 in order to obtain the number 11,732.45

$11.73245 \times 1,000 = 11,732.45$

22) Choice D is correct

factor of 30 = {1, 2, 3, 5, 6, 10, 15, 30}, 16 is not a factor of 30.

23) Choice C is correct

Let's review the choices provided.

A. $30 \times 3 = 90$

B. $45 \times 3 = 135$

C. $55 \times 3 = 165$

D. $70 \times 3 = 210$

From choices provided, only 165 is greater than 160 and less than 190.

24) Choice C is correct

Two Angles are supplementary when they add up to 180 degrees. $145° + 35° = 180°$

25) Choice A is correct

$\frac{25}{100} \times 24 = 6$

www.EffortlessMath.com

... So Much More Online!

✓ FREE Math lessons

✓ More Math learning books!

✓ Mathematics Worksheets

✓ Online Math Tutors

Need a PDF version of this book?

Send email to: info@EffortlessMath.com

Made in the USA
Columbia, SC
13 November 2019